The Pastor
as Evangelist

Books by Richard Stoll Armstrong
Published by The Westminster Press

The Pastor as Evangelist
Service Evangelism

The Pastor
as Evangelist

Richard Stoll Armstrong

The Westminster Press
Philadelphia

Book design by Gene Harris

First edition

Published by The Westminster Press®
Philadelphia, Pennsylvania

PRINTED IN THE UNITED STATES OF AMERICA
9 8 7 6 5 4 3 2 1

Library of Congress Cataloging in Publication Data

Armstrong, Richard Stoll, 1924–
    The pastor as evangelist.

    Includes bibliographical references and index.
    1. Evangelistic work. 2. Clergy—Office. I. Title.
BV3793.A75 1984   253.7   84–10359
ISBN 0–664–24556–0 (soft)

To
Ricky

from whom I learned
that spirited sensitivity
is a gift of God,
and whose brief life and death
were part of my preparation
for God's call to ministry

Contents

Foreword

This book is very much needed. It deals with an extremely important but strangely neglected aspect of evangelism. Most books and conferences on evangelism give the pastor the leading role. They make it clear that what the church's members and organizations do to bring others to the Christian faith and fellowship depends most of all on the pastor's leadership. The church rightly counts on the pastor to be the organizer, trainer, director, and continual impeller of evangelism. But very little is said about the pastor's own evangelistic efforts. Richard Armstrong's purpose is to remedy this lack. He moves the field commander out of the safe and remote command post and right into the front lines.

There are good reasons why pastors may feel that working with individuals who are not church members is not how they serve best. For one thing, they lack the contacts. Pastors' working hours and social times are spent mostly with members of their own church. Moreover, pastors may feel they are handicapped as witnesses. They are afraid of sounding like ministers. People already know what a preacher believes! "A jury always discounts a paid witness." Outsiders want to know what the church looks like from the pew, not from the pulpit. So pastors may—perhaps with sorrow, perhaps with relief—come to believe that they can do most not by being just one more personal evangelist but by inspiring and sending out dozens of evangelists, not by talking with just one person at a time but by presenting Christ to hundreds of people, through sermons and talks, in the pulpit and the classroom, at funerals, weddings, and youth assemblies.

But this is a conclusion Dr. Armstrong is not willing to accept. He reminds us that the commandment to "do the work of an evangelist" is addressed to all followers of Christ, including pastors. "Some pastors . . . believe their role and responsibility is to equip others to do the work of an evangelist, rather than their doing it." He challenges the pastor's supposed lack of contacts by pointing to the many opportunities for personal evangelism that pastors can have in the performance of their normal duties, including opportunities with the many persons who seek out a church or its pastor because of some special need.

Those of us who have spent our working lives entirely in schools or churches need the insights that the author has gained from the remarkably wide variety of worlds he has inhabited. A naval officer during World War II, he has also been a minor-league baseball player and front-office executive, the public relations director of two different major-league baseball clubs, the copy and plans director of an advertising agency, a sports commentator and a director and producer of radio and television sports programs, vice-president for development of a major theological seminary, a pastor, and now a seminary professor. He writes music and poetry and in earlier years was an arranger for and member of several different singing groups. What he has experienced in these varied associations has taught him a great deal about how to talk with people about the Christian faith—and how not to. It is this, plus what he has learned as a husband, father, friend, and pastor, that is offered to us in this book.

The author also passes on to his readers much that he has learned as an avid student and ardent advocate of evangelism. He has done wide reading on the subject and has learned from the Bible about the meaning and urgency of evangelism. He is one of the country's most widely sought leaders of conferences and training programs on evangelism, and he has a broad understanding of what is happening in churches through his constant dialogue with the countless pastors and lay people who attend those events. His ten-year pastorate in Philadelphia was the subject of *The Oak Lane Story,* the book and the film that the Division of Evangelism of The United Presbyterian Church U.S.A. used to challenge and inspire churches everywhere to an inclusive outreach in their communities. His congregation's powerful and persistent evangelistic efforts resulted in a church that was truly integrated in all its activities and inclusive in its fellowship.

Dr. Armstrong's theological reflection on his extended pastorates in Philadelphia and Indianapolis, and on his experiences in other churches where he served as an interim preacher for periods of six to eighteen months, resulted in a very thoughtful and pastoral book, *Service Evangelism.* That title reflects his insistence that evangelism should be sensitive to human needs. The church's first concern should be to minister to people's needs, not to add names to the rolls. Thus does the church win the right to be heard. Other motives, including the church's desire to grow and its sense of evangelistic duty, are valid but subordinate.

Although the current volume is compatible with the principles and style of *Service Evangelism,* the author explores in the pages that follow an entirely different aspect of evangelism, focusing on the pastor's own evangelistic ministry. Dr. Armstrong brings to the task a wealth of sound counsel on how ministers may use their personal contacts to open the way to Christian faith and living. He understands a pastor's special handicaps and opportunities. He gives clear and practical advice on how ministers can make the most of familiar situations. There is a valuable chapter on how they can help members of their own families come to a fuller experience of Christ. There is guidance on the ways best suited to friends, strangers, and parishioners and to the different age groups, from childhood to old age. He gives commonsense suggestions, which anyone could have thought of but most of us have not, for the use of the telephone, letters, and broadcasting.

Profound theology is given a down-to-earth immediacy, as in the paradox of faith that God offers us a gift that must be grasped, or the advice that "we should be moving constantly from faith toward knowledge, not the other way around." One of the great strengths of this book is its solid connection with scripture. The author must always be looking for light on evangelism as he reads the Bible. His many quotations give us excit-

ing discoveries of biblical inspiration and guidance for evangelism.

Dr. Armstrong's originality and lucid, straight-out style
make reading pleasant, and his humor makes it enjoyable. His
frequent flashing sentences are illuminating. For example: "Living room sermons are about as appropriate as a tuxedo at a
picnic." "Some of the churchy types who latch on to us ministers make our families want to head in the opposite direction."
"Theology is the church's conversation with itself; evangelism
is the church's conversation with the world." "Pastor-evangelists should be more concerned about how the message gets
through than about how they come across."

The book comes to an impressive conclusion with its chapter
on the pastor's spiritual rewards, whose key assurance is, "The
pastor who strives to do the work of an evangelist will grow in
the effort—spiritually, theologically, and emotionally." The
evangelist always has to be his own or her own first convert.
Someone who is continually thinking hard about how to tell
others of the Christian faith, how to answer questions or respond to doubts, will be coming to a more lively understanding
of Christian truth than could be gained by reading volumes of
theology. Someone who has tried to tell what Christ can mean,
and has spent the next day wondering how better to have said
it, will have grown in the effort. An evangelist who seems to
have failed and has nothing left to try but prayer, and who then
sees the other person come to a joyful, transforming acceptance
of God's love in Christ, will gain a new hold on spiritual reality
by having participated in a miracle.

"Evangelize or fossilize" is an old saying that applies both to
ministers and to congregations. This last chapter declares that
personal evangelism keeps a pastor spiritually alive, theologically growing, and emotionally healthy. It gives power to one's
entire ministry—in the pulpit, in counseling, in comforting, in
everything. Seen from the other side, these are the benefits a
pastor who is not an evangelist will lose.

That is a powerful conclusion to a very important book.

GEORGE E. SWEAZEY

Preface

One painful conclusion I reached long ago and have not had reason to modify, after many years of trying to help churches accept and fulfill their ministry of evangelism, is that the bottleneck in the process is often if not usually the pastor. It may be theoretically possible, but it is highly improbable that any congregation of a so-called mainline denomination will accept its corporate evangelistic responsibility without the active leadership, support, and involvement of the pastor.

To be sure, lay women and men can bear witness to Christ as individuals, whether or not their church has an organized evangelism program. A church, furthermore, may even be growing numerically without doing evangelism. The relationship between church growth and evangelism is one we shall explore later. For now, suffice it to say that a conscious ministry of outreach to the unchurched, including a persistent, consistent, well-conceived, and well-coordinated visitation program, is unlikely to occur without the pastor's enthusiastic encouragement and direction.

In the courses I have taught and the workshops and seminars I have conducted over the years, I have been probing the hang-ups and concerns of hundreds of pastors regarding various aspects of evangelism. Although many of their concerns are legitimate, and all of their concerns are important to those who have them, there is no valid excuse for any pastor to deny or refuse his or her own ministry of evangelism. That conviction is the reason for this book, which is an appeal and a challenge to pastors to look at their ministry through evangelistic glasses. The focus, as the title indicates, is on the pastor as evangelist.

The reader will note that I use the terms "pastor as evangelist" and "pastor-evangelist" interchangeably, according to the context.

Admittedly, this is one person's point of view, and there is no claim to infallibility or to universality for the contents of these pages. There is the important matter of pastoral style, which obviously informs and colors all that one has to say about ministry. How one does evangelism in a given setting or situation is open to discussion; that a pastor should do the work of an evangelist is not, in my opinion, debatable. The question is not whether but how to be a pastor-evangelist. I shall attempt, nevertheless, to make the case for accepting the role, because there may be some who are unwilling to grant me that assumption.

I am deeply grateful to my friend and colleague George E. Sweazey for his foreword to this book and to my students at Princeton Theological Seminary for being the sounding board for many of the ideas contained herein. I am also indebted to the innumerable pastors and lay persons who helped convince me of the need to address the topic, and most of all to my wife, Margie, whose constant encouragement and perceptive comments have been an indispensable part of the entire project.

R. S. A.

Princeton, New Jersey

1
The Pastor's Evangelistic Concerns

In the seminars for pastors we always start with a time for sharing their personal needs and concerns regarding evangelism. We list these on a blackboard or a sheet of newsprint, not only as a visible reminder of both the diversity and the similarity of their interests but also as a checklist for a relevant and realistic agenda. I wish I had made copies of more of those lists over the years, but I have retrieved as many as I could find, in order to confirm or contradict with some statistical evidence my general impressions.

The categorizing of these voluntary responses is somewhat arbitrary, inasmuch as individual expressions vary and there will obviously be much overlapping. What I am classifying is the verbalized feelings of several hundred pastors, not their replies to a multiple-choice questionnaire. Nor can I accurately identify and categorize the respondents by denominational affiliation, as the lists did not include that information. The constituencies of most of the groups were ecumenical, although some seminars were composed primarily of pastors of one denomination, such as Methodists, Episcopalians, Presbyterians, Moravians, or Disciples. While I do not have any statistical evidence to prove the point, I have not noticed any significant variances in the concerns of pastors of different denominations. To be sure, there were often unique emphases in terms of denominational goals and objectives. A Mennonite group, for example, wanted to look at evangelism in the light of the impact of urbanization on their traditionally rural ministry. A gathering of Anglican priests spent two weeks exploring a suitable approach to evangelism for their diocese. But almost any group of theologically trained pastors will have pretty much the same concerns. I could almost list them in advance. Only the wording changes.

Pastors, like lay people, attend seminars for different reasons. Some come by choice, perhaps as part of their continuing education; some are there under duress, perhaps because their church board or senior minister told them to come. Regardless of their motivation, collectively they usually reflect the gamut of stereotypical attitudes and levels of understanding one would expect to encounter in a group discussion of any controversial theological issue.

And evangelism is controversial! The word itself is a red flag for many. It is not that they are opposed to the proclamation of the gospel. What bothers them is the way it is done, and by whom. They question the propriety in a pluralistic society of what they deem to be an overly aggressive evangelistic approach by some churches. They would describe themselves as evangelical, but they are suspicious of evangelicals. It is the noun, not the adjective, that bothers them. They bring to the seminar their own image of what evangelism is and what it should be. I can never assume any general agreement in their operating assumptions, or a common understanding of the basic vocabulary of evangelism, or unanimity of purpose, or total concurrence as to what the agenda should be. All this must be sorted out before any real communication can take place.

In view of the divergent needs and varied (even at times conflicting) expectations with which the participants come to such a seminar, it is not at all surprising that the largest number (30.9 percent) of questions in the sample shown in Appendix A have to do with the meaning of evangelism. It is not that the questioners do not have their own definition of evangelism; they want to know what other people think it is—and then argue about it! Is there one definition, on which everyone can agree, one which precludes their perjorative image of how other people do evangelism? As pastors they have come in search of an adequate theology and a viable style of evangelism for the contemporary church in a pluralistic world, which appears to be on a toboggan slide toward self-destruction. What is the gospel for such a world? they ask. What is the relationship between evangelism and the stewardship of all of life? These kinds of questions I have classified as relating to the pastors' understanding of evangelism.

Another group (16.2 percent) of concerns have to do with the pastors' feelings about their own involvement in evangelism. Some wonder how to increase their personal commitment to evangelism or how to deal with their own negative attitude toward it. Others are concerned about their own spirituality. Many want to know how to share their faith with integrity, or how to communicate their faith better. Quite a few confess their fear of doing evangelism or their inability to motivate others to do it. Some want clarification as to the pastor's role, wondering if it is not to equip others for evangelism, rather than doing it oneself.

The two categories mentioned so far have in common the fact that they both relate to the pastor's personal wrestling match with evangelism, whether in terms of understanding or of attitude. Together they constitute 47.1 percent of the responses, verifying what I have long known to be true: that is, that a surprisingly large number of pastors have all kinds of personal hang-ups about evangelism. Add to these another 9.9 percent who express concerns about their own pastoral skills, and the total number of responses relating to the pastors' personal evangelism jumps to 57 percent! These are the responses of those who came to seminars. What are we to think about the pastors who would never attend an evangelism seminar or read a book like this? I suspect it is not because they are experts! It is more likely apathy or antipathy that keeps them at arm's length from evangelism. There are even those who believe the word should be expunged from the Christian vocabulary!

It is to be expected that the majority of those who do attend a training event come for the purpose of acquiring new ideas or skills, not to argue about the topic. More than half of the needs expressed by the participants, including the 9.9 percent just mentioned, are of a practical nature, reflecting the assumption that evangelism is not an optional ministry of the church. Irrespective of when or how they may have adopted the premise, for them evangelism is a given. They are there to share ideas that will be useful in their ministries. I have grouped their needs under the following categories: Equipping and Motivating Church Members (20.8 percent), Evangelism Programs for the Local Church (11.4 percent), Reaching the Unchurched (5.7 percent), Ministering to Inactive Members (5.1 percent), and Concerns About Pastoral Skills (9.9 percent). It was difficult sometimes to decide whether a particular response belonged more appropriately in one category or another. An evangelism program for the local church, for example, includes strategies for motivating and equipping church members, and a program for community outreach includes a concern for the unchurched. My principle was to try to classify the responses on the basis of what seemed to be their *predominant* emphasis or concern.

The figures in Appendix A do not represent a one-to-one correlation between the number of pastors and the number of responses, as there were considerably more of the former than of the latter. There are two main reasons for the disparity: (1) not everyone verbalized a concern, and (2) some echoed the concerns expressed by others, in which case nothing was added to the list. Had I been thinking at the time that I would ever be doing a numerical breakdown, I would have noted the number of times a particular concern was repeated. What the figures do show is the relative frequency with which the different concerns appear on the lists I happened to save. They are, as the heading of Appendix A indicates, only a sample, but adequate to provide what I believe is a fairly accurate picture of what most pastors are thinking about evangelism these days.

Another way of looking at the picture is provided by a word-association exercise that I have used with pastors and with seminary students in some of my courses. Sometimes on the very first day I write the word "Evangelism" on the blackboard and ask them what other words come to mind. What I am looking for is their top-of-the-head reaction. After a few minutes I put a different heading on the board. "Evangelism and You," and ask them, without any discussion, "Now what words come to mind?" Interestingly, the second list is noticeably different from the first. Still without any discussion, I write a third heading, "Evangelism and the Average Church Member." The heading always prompts some interesting responses from the class, again very different from the first two lists, as can be seen in the lists in Appendix B. These were compiled from several different groups of seminary students and ministers representing a variety of nationalities, denominational affiliations, theological perspectives, church experience, and racial, ethnic, linguistic, and cultural backgrounds. As was mentioned above, many of the words occurred over and over again, but they are listed only once.

The lists reveal that ministers and seminary students tend to be less positive about themselves as evangelists than they are about evangelism per se, and they are least positive in their impressions of "the average church member." The number of words with negative overtones is greater in column two than in column one, and greater in column three than in column two. Students and pastors alike never fail to express their belief that many if not most church members consider evangelism to be the pastor's job. Pastors tend to think their responsibility is to equip their members to be evangelists. There is much truth in both opinions!

Not all church members are as ready to rest the burden of responsibility for evangelism solely on the shoulders of the pastor as some pastors think they are. Many (perhaps even most) dedicated, intelligent lay people realize that the task is theirs as well. They have their opinions, however, as to what their pastors should be doing. It may be constructive for some pastors to know what those opinions are. Here is a summary of the responses of a large group of lay men and women at a recent evangelism training seminar to the question "What do you consider to be the pastor's responsibility in the church's evangelistic ministry?"

Preaching	Words used to describe what preaching should be included significant, spiritual, good, thought-provoking, gospel-filled, biblical, invitational, appealing for commitment
Worship	The most common suggestion was "Make the worship experience meaningful for visiting worshipers"; other words were recognize, welcome, involve, invite, enthuse

Education	The general consensus was that the pastor should "educate the congregation regarding evangelism through sermons, training events, programs, one-on-one conversations," etc., and "teach the Bible!"
Sense of mission	"The pastor should spearhead the creation of a mission statement for the church, including evangelism; it is the pastor's responsibility to inspire and educate the congregation regarding mission"
Calling	"The pastor should make personal contact with every prospective member and should call on inactive members!"

When the lay people had finished expressing themselves, I asked the pastors who were present to comment on the list. Surprisingly, they agreed with what had been said. Perhaps they were intimidated by the presence of some of their own members and were embarrassed to admit any disagreement. For whatever reason, the pastors in that group by their acquiescence were publicly acknowledging that the weight of the responsibility for equipping the church to be the evangelist was theirs.

And so it is! The question is, How are they fulfilling that responsibility? It is my firm conviction that one cannot fulfill it very well unless one not only is an equipper or enabler of others but is also, oneself, an evangelist. In the chapters that follow we shall discuss in what sense and in what ways a pastor should and can fulfill that role effectively and with integrity.

2
The Pastor's Understanding of Evangelism

What is evangelism? Because, as we have seen, so many pastors have questions about the meaning of evangelism, this seems the logical place to begin. But this is also where the trouble begins, as there are as many definitions of evangelism as there are definers!

THE MEANING

In the most precise sense, evangelism is the proclamation of the gospel. The word "evangel" is a transliteration of the Greek word *euaggelion,* translated *gospel,* which is a contraction of the Anglo-Saxon term *godspell,* meaning good tidings or good news. The New Testament evangel referred either to the good news that Jesus preached (the proclamation of the kingdom of God) or to the good news about Jesus, who was both the announcer and the revelation of the kingdom.

The New Testament verb *euaggelizesthai* means to bring or to proclaim the gospel, specifically the good news of Jesus Christ. Strictly speaking, John R. W. Stott is correct in his insistence that evangelism should be defined solely in terms of its message, not its target (i.e., the recipients of the message), or its results (i.e., whether or not people are converted), or the methods used (i.e., how it is done).[1] It does not seem, however, that many who speak are speaking strictly. Most definers include far more than the mere equation of evangelism with proclamation. Writers on the subject are not content to let it go at that. Their "definitions" usually sound more like descriptions, as illustrated by the following quotations taken from a list which I have been collecting for many years.

1. "Evangelism is making the gospel known to those who do not know it, in hope that they may be turned to God in faith, and making it more effectively known to those who already know it within the Church, that their faith may grow in clarity and strength" (Special Commission on Evangelism appointed by the General Board of the National Council of the Churches of Christ in the U.S.A.).

2. "That is precisely what evangelism is. It is the decisive confrontation of persons[2] with the gospel in Jesus Christ to the end that they may believe in him and believing find salvation in his service" (from a statement published in 1959 by the Department on Studies in Evangelism of the World Council of Churches entitled "A Theological Reflection on the Work of Evangelism").

3. "To evangelize is so to present Christ Jesus in the power of the Holy Spirit, that [people] shall come to put their trust in God through him, to accept him as their Saviour, and serve him as their King in the fellowship of his Church" (Archbishops' Committee of Inquiry on the Evangelistic Work of the Church, adopted in 1918 and reaffirmed in 1945 in the Report of the Commission on Evangelism appointed by the Archbishops of Canterbury and York entitled "Towards the Conversion of England").

4. "The fundamental meaning and aim of all evangelism— to tell the good news of Jesus in such a way as to elicit a response of faith which will be sealed in an act of commitment (baptism in the case of the unbaptized) and membership in the Christian community. But the heart of evangelism is the initial act of confronting someone else with Jesus" (Douglas Webster, *What Is Evangelism?*, 1961).

5. "Evangelism strictly speaking is the proclamation or presentation of the gospel of Jesus Christ to persons in this secular age so that they will understand its crucial and relevant significance and respond to him as Lord and Savior in faith and

obedience, identify themselves with the Christian community, and serve him in daily life and relationship" (Elmer G. Homrighausen, *Rethinking the Great Commission in an Age of Revolution,* 1968).

6. "What is evangelism but the sharing of the good news? Love and acceptance and forgiveness and hope—that good news made incarnate in Jesus Christ" (George Peters, "Evangelism Now," *Presbyterian Life,* June 1972).

7. "Evangelism is every possible way of reaching outside the church to make contacts with definite persons, to cultivate their knowledge of Christian faith and living, to lead them to confess Christ as their Lord and Savior, to bring them into church membership, and to help them commence Christian habits and church participation" (George E. Sweazey, *The Church as Evangelist,* 1978).

8. "Evangelism is more than the mere proclamation of evangelical truth. It is the winning of individual men and women for Jesus Christ, with all that means in reshaping outlook and character" (D. Patrick Thomson, *Aspects of Evangelism,* 1968).

9. "Genuine evangelism therefore is the proclamation of Jesus as Savior and Lord, who gave his life for others and wants us to do likewise, setting us free by declaring God's forgiveness. Evangelism is true and credible only when it is both word and deed, proclamation and witness. To say this is not to suggest that evangelism derives its power from the good deeds of Christians; our failures in obedience, however, can act as stumbling blocks" (Section Report of the World Conference on Mission and Evangelism at Melbourne, 1980).

10. "To evangelize is to spread the good news that Jesus Christ died for our sins and was raised from the dead according to the scriptures, and that as reigning Lord he now offers the forgiveness of sins and the liberating gift of the Spirit to all who repent and believe. Our Christian presence in the world is indispensable to evangelism and so is that kind of dialogue whose

purpose is to listen sensitively in order to understand. But evangelism itself is the proclamation of the historical, biblical Christ as Savior and Lord, with a view to persuading people to come to him personally, and so be reconciled to God. In issuing the gospel invitation we have no liberty to conceal the cost of discipleship. Jesus still calls all who would follow him to deny themselves, take up their cross, and identify themselves with his new community. The results of evangelism include obedience to Christ, incorporation into his Church, and responsible service to the world" (Lausanne Conference on World Evangelism, 1974).

11. Evangelism is "proclaiming the good news of salvation to men and women with a view to their conversion to Christ and incorporation into his Church" (Michael Green, *Evangelism in the Early Church,* 1970).

12. "To evangelize is to communicate the gospel in such a way that men and women have a valid opportunity to accept Jesus Christ as Lord and Saviour and become responsible members of the Church" (Edward R. Dayton and David A. Fraser, *Planning Strategies for World Evangelization,* 1980).

13. "Evangelism is the linking of human life to the story of Jesus Christ" (Emilio Castro, in an address given at the Overseas Ministries Study Center, Ventnor, New Jersey, 1981).

14. "The evangelical commitment of the Church . . . must be like Christ's—an engagement with the poorest. . . . God takes their defense and loves them. This is why the poor are the first addressees of mission and their evangelization is *par excellence* the sign of the mission of Jesus. . . . This commitment to the poor —a sign of authenticity—demands the conversion of the whole Church in view of their total liberation" (quoted by Mortimer Arias in *The Cry of My People,* from Puebla Documents Nos. 1134–1152 by the Roman Catholic Bishops, 1979).

15. "Evangelism is the good news of the great victory of God, his accession, his kingly rule, the dawn of the new age" (Harvie M. Conn, *Bible Studies on World Evangelization and the Simple Life Style,* 1981).

16. "The evangelical goal is a redeemed humanity. . . . The Church's abiding task, its timeless imperative through the ages, is to give luminous expression to the gospel. This demands that the Church be sensitive to the human situation in each successive period of history and to the need to make the gospel's changeless essence meaningful in a changing world. If this is to be achieved, evangelism must be given fresh significance and vitality. It must not confine itself to communicating the gospel; it must apply the gospel to all of life. Individual Christians and the Christian community as a whole have the crucial responsibility of confronting people everywhere, in a discreet but decisive way, with the reality of Christ and of facing the varied problems of human society in the light and power of Christ" (John A. Mackay, "Toward an Evangelical Renaissance," *Christianity Today,* February 4, 1972).

17. "Evangelism is the act of so presenting the gospel of God which is revealed in Christ that people are persuaded to commit themselves to his purpose. They are drawn into the community of his servant people by whom he is at work to extend his kingdom. Such evangelism is the heart of mission, even though not the whole of it, since mission is the totality of the Church's participation in God's action in the world. Evangelism is precisely the enlistment of persons in such participation" (David M. Stowe, *Ecumenicity and Evangelism,* 1970).

18. "The ministry by which a congregation shares The Faith, makes new disciples, and thereby becomes contagious is called 'evangelism,' or sometimes 'evangelization.' . . . Whatever else one might mean by evangelism, one must necessarily mean the 'making of new disciples' " (George G. Hunter III, *The Contagious Congregation,* 1979; Dr. Hunter elaborates extensively on these statements in his first chapter).

19. "To evangelize is to invite persons to trust the love and mercy of Christ. To evangelize is to ask persons to place themselves under the sovereignty of Christ as loyal subjects. . . . An authentic evangelism will call for full faith in Christ which is trustful of his grace and loyal to his service. It will do this in ways that are appropriate to the needs and respectful of the

rights of each person" (John R. Hendrick, *Opening the Door of Faith,* 1977).

20. "Evangelism is being, doing, and telling the gospel of the kingdom of God, in order that by the power of the Holy Spirit persons and structures may be converted to the lordship of Jesus Christ" (Delos Miles, *Introduction to Evangelism,* 1983).

As one scans the foregoing list, one notes that the definitions, which come from a variety of sources, do not conform to the limitation demanded by John Stott. It seems that almost everyone who writes on the subject either explicitly or implicitly includes something about the purpose and intended results, and often something about methodology. Even the oft-quoted statement by D. T. Niles, "Evangelism is one beggar telling another beggar where to get food," implies far more than the mere proclamation of the gospel. So does the familiar dictum "Evangelism is bringing Christ to people and people to Christ." The succinctness of these two statements and others like them is deceiving. They say more than they appear to say.

But they do not say everything, or even enough, when compared to the statements on the list. If all one had to go on was D. T. Niles's metaphor (and if that were all he said about it!), one would hardly know from that what evangelism is.[3] The saying is true but not adequate. It is clever but not complete. One wants to say, after hearing it, Yes, evangelism is that, but it is not only that.

Perhaps the best way to approach the task of defining evangelism is to accept the most literal definition and then add whatever descriptive statements are necessary to convey one's understanding of the term. If evangel means good news, then we must agree with Stott that evangelism, strictly speaking, is the proclamation of the good news. At this point some distinctions need to be made.

Evangelism and Evangelization

These two words are often, though improperly, used synonymously. Evangelization implies a recipient, a personal object. To evangelize is to preach or proclaim the gospel *to* someone. It also implies a result. To say someone has been evangelized means that person has been converted or brought into the church. Evangelization includes evangelism, but evangelism does not necessarily include (i.e., result in) evangelization. In that sense, Urban T. Holmes was right in arguing that evangelism is the narrower of the two words. For that reason he opted for the word evangelization as "an on-going action within the total life of the Church."[4] The choice of words depends upon what one wants to say, and it behooves the user to know the connotations of each.

Evangelism and Church Growth

One of the problems with the term "church growth" is that a commonly used expression has been given a specific application. So we now have a Church Growth Movement, which has given its own definition to the term:

> The term "church growth" is a McGavranism. At first McGavran attempted to phrase the insights he had developed using more traditional language such as "evangelism" or "missions," but he soon found that these terms were little more than useless. They had been defined and redefined so much that they had lost their cutting edge. When "evangelism" and "missions" came to mean everything good that Christians did individually and collectively, they then meant practically nothing.
>
> So in order to describe, in a precise way, what he was trying to articulate, Donald McGavran took two common words and welded them together. . . . Actually "church growth" means all that is involved in bringing men and women who do not have a personal relationship to Jesus Christ into fellowship with him and into responsible church membership.[5]

That sounds like a definition of evangelism! Indeed, the use of the expression as a substitute (euphemism?) for evangelism has blurred the relationship between the two terms. They should not be used interchangeably. The hope, of course, is that evangelism will result in church growth. But depending upon other factors, church growth may take place with or without any evangelistic outreach by the church. Some churches grow because of and some in spite of the kind of evangelism they do. The confusion arises when the principles of the Church Growth Movement are substituted for the principles of evangelism. The emphasis on numerical growth and statistical success may cause a church to compromise its theological integrity.[6] One can hardly be opposed to church growth, but the pursuit of that goal should not be at the expense of a watered-down gospel proclaimed by a church that has lost its prophetic vision and voice. The church is called not to be successful but to be faithful to the Lord, who bids us to deny ourselves and to take up our cross and follow him.

It is true, as C. Peter Wagner and other Church Growth spokespersons have reminded us, that one of the signs of a growing church is a proven evangelistic program.[7] We also need to remember that evangelism is a ministry; church growth is a goal. They are related but not identical. It is disturbing to hear of a multiple-staff church in which an associate or assistant pastor is given the title Minister of Evangelism and Church Growth. Church growth is not a ministry! The title suggests that the individual who holds it is responsible for the growth of the church, which expectation is totally unrealistic if not impossible. There are too many factors beyond the control of any associate minister to hold him or her responsible for the growth of the church. Perhaps the church officers feel they need someone whom they can hold accountable for a declining membership. Or maybe the pastor needs a scapegoat. That is exactly what the Minister of Evangelism and Church Growth may become, if things are not going well. There are circumstances under which no individual could cause a church to grow, not even the pastor. The negative criticism of a vocal minority can frustrate the most enthusiastic efforts of a competent pastor. A divided congregation is never conducive to church growth. Nor is an ineffective pastor, no matter how capable the assistant responsible for church growth.

Another sign of a growing church, according to Peter Wagner, is strong pastoral leadership.[8] That is undoubtedly true, although there may be some debate about what constitutes strong pastoral leadership. It is not the only sign, but it is probably the most obvious one. In my opinion it is the most important one. A word of caution needs to be added, however. While strong pastoral leadership may be a necessary condition, it is not a guarantee. Church growth may not take place without it, but it will not necessarily take place with it. How, then, can any one individual, especially one who is not the head of staff, be held solely responsible for the growth of a church?

That is true even in smaller churches, where it would seem that the pastor should single-handedly be able to "make things happen." Even here, however, it is best to be humble about such matters, for the one ultimately responsible is God, who can frustrate our ambitious programs and clever techniques, as well as redeem our inadequate efforts and surprise us in our discouragements.

Just as it is unfair to blame any one individual for a church's decline (unless, of course, that person is guilty of some egregious misconduct), so it is improper for anyone to take credit for a church's growth. There are simply too many circumstances beyond the control of any one individual. These include the institutional and contextual factors described in the reports of the Hartford Seminary Foundation symposium on church growth and decline.[9] According to Dean Hoge and David Roozen, local contextual factors have a greater effect on church growth than local institutional factors. "The contextual factors explain about 50 to 75 percent, as an estimate, while the institutional factors explain about 30 to 50 percent."[10] The local contextual factors that affect mainline Protestant church growth most powerfully are "affluence of the community, presence of middle-class residential neighborhoods near the church, percent [of] home owners near the church, absence of minorities in the neighborhood, and absence of other Protestant churches nearby."[11] Others included pastoral leadership as one of the significant factors.

No discussion of the relationship between evangelism and church growth would be complete without some reference to the two most controversial principles of the Church Growth Movement. One is the much-debated homogeneous unit principle, stemming from the observation of Donald McGavran that people "like to become Christians without crossing racial, linguistic or class barriers."[12] Writes Peter Wagner, "Of all the scientific hypotheses developed within the Church Growth framework, this one as nearly as any approaches a law."[13] What Church Growth critics object to is not the accuracy of the observation but the evangelistic conclusion that churches should therefore seek first their own kind. Evangelism, they would argue, should be color-blind and class-blind. Should not the love of Jesus Christ transcend all human barriers? My own experience as a pastor confirms that it does. It may be more difficult and time-consuming to win those who are "not like us," but it can be done, and it is worth the effort! The result is an exciting church, one that has discovered that the truest and best homogeneity is not racial, social, or even linguistic, but spiritual.

The second point of issue with the Church Growth Movement has to do with its underplaying of the social gospel. One of Peter Wagner's seven signs of a growing church is for it to have its priorities arranged in biblical order. So far so good. The bone of contention is the fact that social action is excluded from the order. Priority No. 1, according to Wagner, is Commitment to Jesus Christ. What pastor would argue with that? Wagner's second priority is Commitment to the Body of Christ. Most pastors would have no argument with that either, unless it was used as an excuse for never getting to Priority No. 3, which is Commitment to the Work of Christ. For Wagner, subpriority No. 1 under Commitment to the Work of Christ is Evangelism, including local evangelism and worldwide mission. Subpriority No. 2 (notice how far down the list!) is what Wagner calls Social Involvement. Sub-subpriority (a) under Social Involvement is Social Service. Wagner makes a sharp distinction between social service and social action, which he does not believe should be a priority for churches *qua* churches at all. "To the degree that socially involved churches become engaged in social action, as distinguished from social service, they can expect church growth to diminish."[14]

Wagner's controvertible assertion is not clearly supported by the findings of the Hartford Seminary Foundation study of church growth and decline, nor by a study of 97 thriving congregations conducted by the Vocation Agency of the pre-reunion United Presbyterian Church U.S.A.[15] It is helpful to distinguish between the church's ministry of compassion to persons and the church's prophetic ministry to society, which includes its responsibility to address the issues, problems, needs, and systemic evils that affect people's lives. At the same time, I must add that I do not believe the distinction between social service and social action is always as clear as Peter Wagner and others imply. When the love of Christ constrains church members to reach out to others across racial lines, for instance, that church is involved in social action, because it is dealing with what continues to be one of the major social challenges of our North American society, a challenge neither secular society nor the church has met. The concept of homogeneous congregations and the deemphasizing of social action are not helping to solve the problem; they provide a convenient rationalization for churches to maintain their class consciousness and ignore their Christian responsibility. If my experience did not contradict both principles, my Christian conscience would.

One should be aware of the evolution that has taken place in Church Growth thinking, which has become more palatable to its critics as their justifiable concerns have been heard and incorporated. Thus Peter Wagner in a more recent book declares, "Part of a high quality church is to be significantly involved in ministry to the poor and downtrodden. Christian social responsibility cannot be neglected. Too often in the recent past, evangelical churches especially have been negligent in this area of their duty."[16]

Another later and more theologically balanced of the Church Growth offerings is a book by British author Eddie Gibbs entitled *I Believe in Church Growth*. Gibbs does not subscribe totally to the concept of a homogeneous congregation, for he believes the church should be an example to the world of the unity and diversity of the body of Christ, rather than a reflection of the divisions of society. "If the gospel has truly brought reconciliation and mutual appreciation," he writes, "then the local church should demonstrate the reality of this theological truth in practical terms as a testimony to the community."[17] As a corrective to what he sees as an overemphasis on numerical growth in the early years of the Church Growth Movement, Gibbs acknowledges that church enrollment is not to be uncritically equated with a genuine turning to Christ. The heart of the gospel is Jesus Christ, not the church, though he firmly believes that church growth is on God's agenda.

Gibbs also represents a biblically sound corrective to what many Church Growth detractors perceive to be a lopsided theology. He insists that because reconciliation has both a vertical and a horizontal dimension, the gospel must be both personal and social. "Repentance includes turning away from social as well as personal sins. Salvation is not simply individualistic and otherworldly."[18] Noting a lack of emphasis on the kingdom of God in most Church Growth literature, Gibbs wrestles with the paradoxical nature of the kingdom, appealing for a proper awareness of the tension between the growth of the church and the realization of the kingdom. Too great an identification of the two leads to ecclesiastical deification and denominational aggrandizement, while their disassociation "breaks the nerve-cord of hope and destroys the community of commitment to Christ as Saviour and Lord."[19] Gibbs points also to the movement's failure to distinguish between the church and the churches, and to its overlooking of the ambiguities of human existence and the demonic possibilities of all human institutions, including churches, whose missionary efforts are often seen as dehumanizing imperialism.[20]

Eddie Gibbs's book is representative of the later Church Growth writings and is a reason for critics of the movement to mollify their stance and gain from its valid insights.[21] If there are some aspects of theology or methodology with which they disagree, there are many other programmatic ideas and principles from which they could greatly benefit. Church Growth and evangelism are not identical; neither are they antithetical. The better part of wisdom is not to reject in toto the theories and concepts which so many have found helpful, but to use the ideas that are compatible to one's own theology and style. In other words, be selective, no matter whose or which program you are examining. Let us affirm what we can affirm about those whose ideas and ways may be different from ours, so that we all may learn from one another, and so that evangelism and church growth may be compatible partners rather than competitive rivals in the Christian enterprise.[22]

Evangelism, Mission, and Ministry

Ministry means service. Jesus came to minister. "I am among you," he said, "as one who serves" (Luke 22:27). He came not to be served but to serve, or, as the King James Version puts it, "not to be ministered unto, but to minister" (Matt. 20:28; Mark 10:45). The ministry of the church, therefore, is its Christlike service to people, all that it does for people in the name and spirit of Christ, including the sharing of the good news. Evangelism is a form of ministry, its specific function being the proclamation and promulgation of the gospel. Mission conveys the idea of being sent, from the Latin *mitto, mittere, missum,* to send. "As thou didst send me into the world," Jesus prayed, "so I have sent them into the world" (John 17:18). The mission of the church is the ministry it is sent into the world to do. Mission is ministry (service), but not all ministry is mission. The ministry of evangelism is part of the mission of the church. Mission is the more inclusive of the two terms, which are related but not identical. The apostle Paul reminds us that "there are varieties of ministry [*diakoniōn*], but the same Lord" (1 Cor. 12:5).

Paul includes evangelists in his enumeration of vocational roles in Ephesians 4:11, which passage suggests that evangelism is a function of a specific office of the church. Some are evangelists, others are not. This was the view of Genevan Reformer John Calvin, who had very little to say about evangelism. In Calvin's *Institutes of the Christian Religion,* the one passage in which the office is discussed is worth noting:

> Those who preside over the government of the Church, according to the institution of Christ, are named by Paul, first, *Apostles;* secondly, *Prophets;* thirdly, *Evangelists;* fourthly, *Pastors;* and

lastly, *Teachers* (Eph. 4:11). Of these, only the two last have an ordinary office in the Church. The Lord raised up the other three at the beginning of his kingdom, and still occasionally raises them up when the necessity of the times requires. The nature of the apostolic function is clear from the command, "Go ye into all the world, and preach the gospel to every creature" (Mark 16:15). No fixed limits are given them, but the whole world is assigned to be reduced under obedience of Christ, that by spreading the gospel as widely as they could, they might everywhere erect his kingdom. ... The apostles, therefore, were sent forth to bring back the world from its revolt to the true obedience of God, and everywhere establish his kingdom by preaching the gospel; or, if you choose, they were like the first architects of the Church, to lay its foundations throughout the world. ... By *Evangelists,* I mean those who, while inferior in rank to the apostles, were next them in office, and even acted as their substitutes. Such were Luke, Timothy, Titus, and the like; perhaps, also, the seventy disciples whom our Saviour appointed in the second place to the apostles (Luke 10:1). According to this interpretation, which appears to me consonant both to the words and the meaning of Paul, those three functions were not instituted in the Church to be perpetual, but only to endure so long as churches were to be transferred from Moses to Christ; although I deny not, that afterward God occasionally raised up Apostles, or at least Evangelists, in their stead, as has been done in our time. For such were needed to bring back the Church from the revolt of Antichrist. The office I nevertheless call extraordinary, because it has no place in churches duly constituted.[23]

By that last statement, Calvin must have been thinking of the office in relation to church members. He obviously was not thinking about the non-Christian world. His point needs to be addressed, nevertheless. If evangelism is the function of a particular office, is it then the responsibility solely of those who hold the office? There are those who today have been set apart to the office of Evangelist by their particular denomination. There are others, like Billy Graham, called by the Holy Spirit to various evangelistic ministries. The ministry of evangelism, however, belongs not just to gifted individuals but to the whole church, and there is something every member of the body of Christ, including pastors, can do to help the church fulfill that ministry.[24] The question this book will attempt to address is: In what sense is the pastor an evangelist? For now, it is enough to say that it is not a matter of a separate office in the church but of a role that every pastor should fill along with her or his other roles. Our focus is the pastor *as* evangelist. The pastor's evangelistic activity should not be limited to the pulpit. Rather, it has a bearing on almost everything one does in the name of Christ, just as the evangelistic activity of the early Christians informed and involved all that the church was called to be and do in its worship *(leitourgia),* fellowship *(koinōnia),* and service *(diakonia).*

Evangelism and Social Action

We have already discussed the Church Growth attitude toward social action and the distinction it makes between social action and social service. A further word needs to be said about the relationship between social action and evangelism. Lesslie Newbigin has put it cogently:

> Any critic of traditional styles of evangelism can easily point to examples of conversion which are not merely irrelevant but actually counterproductive in relation to the real ethical issues of the time and place. It is notorious that the times and places from which successful evangelistic campaigns and mass conversions have been reported have often been marked by flagrant evils such as racism, militant sectarianism, and blind support of oppressive economic and political systems. How are we to evaluate a form of evangelism which produces baptized, communicant, Bible-reading, and zealous Christians who are committed to church growth but uncommitted to radical obedience to the plain teaching of the Bible on the issues of human dignity and social justice? And how can we defend a form of evangelism which has nothing to say about the big issues of public righteousness and talks only of questions of personal and domestic behavior?[25]

Evangelism and social action are separate but related aspects of the mission of the church. They should not be allowed to become substitutes for each other. Rather they are partners in

mission, as John Stott has described them.[26] Yet the dichotomy
between the two should-be partners persists, regrettably, and
there are still those who want to put themselves and others into
one camp or the other. The relationship between evangelism and
social action is not either/or but both/and. Although that
should be obvious, it cannot be taken for granted that the part-
nership is understood and accepted, especially by those who are
inclined to stress one side or the other.

The church that is concerned about meeting people's needs
cannot overlook the context in which their lives are lived. A
holistic evangelism, therefore, will relate the gospel to their
social as well as their personal needs, their physical as well as
their spiritual hunger. Pastors should help their parishioners to
develop a balanced understanding of evangelism, so that their
present negative notions, if they have any, will not preclude
their involvement in the church's ministry of evangelism, or
cause them to be critical of or even inimical toward those who
are.[27]

Evangelism and Witnessing

The word "witnessing" has taken on a specific meaning in
Christian parlance. It means to tell one's faith story, or to give
one's personal Christian testimony. Technically, a witness is one
who tells what has been personally seen or heard. Most Christians realize, however, that they witness by what they do as well
as by what they say. To the recipients of our witness, actions do
indeed speak louder than words. In that sense, therefore, we are
witnesses whether we want to be or not. We are not all evangelists, but we are all witnesses. Witnessing can be evangelistic, and
evangelism can include witnessing. They are not mutually exclusive, but they are not the same. I may tell my faith story
without proclaiming the gospel of Christ, and I may proclaim
the gospel without giving my personal testimony. Interpersonal
witnessing and one-on-one evangelism are practically inter-
changeable terms, the way they are used. A church's evangelistic outreach will certainly include much interpersonal
witnessing on the part of those involved.

Evangelism and Proselytizing

I am using the term "proselytizing" in a pejorative sense. In the vernacular it means "sheep stealing." It is evangelism gone wrong. It conveys an arrogant attitude, implies a superior stance, and employs an insensitive style. It is coercive, argumentative, and judgmental. It is motivated by self-interest. Its concern is for converts, not for persons. Its approach is more propositional than incarnational, going there and "unloading" rather than being there and caring. I would appeal for a style of evangelism that scrupulously avoids pressure tactics, one which remembers that the witness must first be a listener, that the task is not to browbeat but to share faith, not to win an argument but to make a friend, not to force but to offer.

In my book *Service Evangelism* I have included a number of other distinctions in an attempt to delineate a style of evangelism that relates the sharing of the good news of Jesus Christ to the meeting of human needs. The title is not meant to imply that service *is* evangelism. Rather, it is evangelism done by a church that recognizes and accepts its role as the servant people of God, who follow in the footsteps of a Lord who came as a suffering Servant. It is an appeal not for a method but for a style. It is a call to be Christ's servants as well as his witnesses, both within and without the walls of the church, people who have a mission to serve the community in whatever ways are appropriate and possible and whose concern stretches from their immediate neighborhood to the most distant parts of the earth.

Evangelism and Manipulation

"You seem to be a really effective witness for Christ, Tom. How do you do it?" If Tom tries to analyze and explain what he does, chances are someone will accuse him of being manipulative. It is a familiar response. As soon as one talks about ways of "winning" people, one exposes oneself to the charge of manipulation. Those who resort to deceitful wiles or play upon people's emotions to gain their objectives are guilty as charged. In evangelism the end does not justify the means,

nor the means the end! Both the end and the means must be true
to and worthy of the gospel of Jesus Christ.

For some people, however, evangelization per se is manipulation. If they are right, then *any* attempt to persuade people to
believe or to do something is manipulative, including preaching,
debating, and political campaigning, not to mention selling and
advertising. Any practitioner of the art of persuasion who employs unscrupulous methods to achieve his or her ends is perni-
ciously manipulative and culpable. But evangelists need not be
and should not be manipulative. If one is open, honest, and
sincere about one's feelings and intentions toward those one is
trying to reach, if one's method and message are not deceptive
or misleading, if one has others' best interests and not one's own
interest at heart, then one cannot be justly accused of being
manipulative, no matter how persuasive one might be. The difference between commendable evangelization and reprehensible
manipulation is the difference between emotion and emotionalism, between persuasion and coercion, between integrity and
expediency. Manipulators are committed to gimmicks, not the
gospel; to what works, not what helps. It is totally unfair, therefore, to accuse an evangelist of being manipulative, simply because she or he is a persuasive communicator.

Evangelism and Faith Sharing

My approach to evangelism and witnessing is based on a
particular understanding of faith, one that takes seriously the
givenness of faith. After wrestling long and hard with the paradoxical nature of faith, the tension between what I have called
"the gift and the grasp,"[28] I have come out on the gift side of
the dichotomy, concluding that ultimately faith is a gift, and the
paradox is really a pseudo paradox. That realization came as the
result of an intense rational process, but with the impact of a
revelation. I had often said and heard it said that faith is a gift,
but I had never thought the statement through to its logical
conclusion. If one takes seriously the givenness of faith, it has
tremendous implications for the way one does evangelism. Faith
is not something I can make myself have but something I find

myself with. How, then, can I make anyone else have it? If God is the Giver of faith, what is the role of the witness or the evangelist? It is not to try to prove the existence of God. I can't prove God even to myself, let alone to anyone else, for I realize that all my reasons are faith statements and my arguments are tautological. The task of the witness is to share the evidence that confirms one's faith assumptions. One can do that with integrity if one's affirmations have a confessional tone, and if one takes to heart what it means to be Christ's woman or Christ's man in the world today.

So my approach to interpersonal witnessing and person-to-person evangelism is a faith-sharing approach. I define faith sharing as a three-way conversation in which people relate to each other their personal experiences of God. I say three-way because the Holy Spirit is also involved. For me, even preaching is a faith-sharing experience, as the preacher proclaims the convictions of faith to the faith community. The communicator realizes that the affirmations of faith are not self-evident to a nonbeliever, or even to some believers. Does that disaffirm the self-authenticating power of the scriptures? No, but it recognizes that to say that the scriptures are self-authenticating is itself a faith statement!

The relationship between faith sharing and evangelism is expressed in the following descriptive definition of service evangelism: "By evangelism I mean reaching out to others in Christian love, identifying with them, caring for them, listening to them, and sharing faith with them in such a way that they will freely respond and want to commit themselves to trust, love, and obey God as a disciple of Jesus Christ and a member of his servant community, the church."[29]

As I have already conceded, that is more of a description than a definition. Like the other definitions listed at the beginning of this chapter, it represents a need to say more about evangelism than merely that it is the proclamation of the gospel. Its purpose is to let others know what I have in mind, when I use the term. It is not presented as the ultimate definition of evangelism. If the reader does not like this one or any of the others on the list, my suggestion is to do what I did: Write your own! Hammer it out in the light of your own theology, doing justice to the kinds of questions with which we have been wrestling in these pages. Having satisfied yourself as to the meaning of evangelism, give thought next to the mandate for doing it.

THE MANDATE

Local congregations have a threefold mandate for mission, a mandate that calls for both the personal and the social dimensions of the gospel.

The Biblical Mandate

There is, first of all, the Great Commission, found in each of the Synoptic Gospels: "Go therefore and make disciples of all nations" (Matt. 28:19); "Go into all the world and preach the gospel to the whole creation" (Mark 16:15); "And that repentance and forgiveness of sins should be preached in his name to all nations. . . . You are witnesses to these things" (Luke 24:47–48). We have already noted the mission emphasis in Jesus' intercessory prayer. Hear his words again in context:

> I have given them thy word; and the world has hated them because they are not of the world, even as I am not of the world. I do not pray that thou shouldst take them out of the world, but that thou shouldst keep them from the evil one. They are not of the world, even as I am not of the world. Sanctify them in the truth; thy word is truth. As thou didst send me into the world, so I have sent them into the world (John 17:14–18).

The last line is echoed in the Johannine version of the Great Commission, when Jesus appeared to the disciples behind closed doors, after his resurrection: "Jesus said to them again, 'Peace be with you. As the Father has sent me, even so I send you' " (John 20:21). There is also the final appearance of Jesus before the ascension, as recorded by Luke in the first chapter of Acts: "You shall receive power when the Holy Spirit has come upon you; and you shall be my witnesses in Jerusalem and in all Judea and Samaria and to the end of the earth" (1:8).

In Jesus' parable of the great banquet the master says to his servant, "Go out to the highways and hedges, and compel people to come in, that my house may be filled" (Luke 14:23). That sounds like a proof text for an aggressive approach. The context makes it clear, however, that the master is underscoring the fact that those who were originally invited and made excuses have lost their chance to come. He would rather have the remaining places filled by reluctant outsiders who have to be persuaded to come than by the original invitees. In any case, the master's command is to reach out. And notice to whom: not to people like the ones on the guest list but to the social misfits. "Go out quickly to the streets and lanes of the city, and bring in the poor and maimed and blind and lame" (v. 21), and after them any street people who are around. The folks attending that banquet were anything but a homogeneous group!

In his second letter to Corinth (5:18–20), Paul reminds us that God has given us the ministry and entrusted to us the message of reconciliation. "So we are ambassadors for Christ, God making his appeal through us" (v. 20). In that same letter he appeals for a style of evangelism that should be a model for all of us. "We are not, like so many, peddlers of God's word; but as men [and women] of sincerity, as commissioned by God, in the sight of God we speak in Christ" (2:17).

There are many other passages that could be cited; those I have chosen are sufficient to establish the biblical mandate for mission.

The Church's Mandate

There is also the mandate laid upon us by the church. Denominations and councils of churches have been exhorting their constituents year after year to give top priority to evangelism. The Governing Board of the National Council of Churches adopted unanimously a policy statement emphasizing the social and corporate as well as the personal nature of Christian commitment, including the following declaration on evangelism:

The task of evangelism today is calling people to repentance, to faith in Jesus Christ, to study God's word, to continue steadfast in prayer, and to bearing witness to him. This is a primary function of the church in its congregational, denominational and ecumenical manifestations. It challenges the most creative capabilities in the churches while at the same time depending upon the Holy Spirit to be the real evangelist.[30]

Similar statements have come from the World Council of Churches:

The authority of the Church to evangelize derives from this authority of Christ and of his Spirit. . . . He summons them to announce the gospel to all [people], whatever their condition. . . . The basic urgency of evangelism arises, therefore, from the nature and content of the gospel itself, and its authority lies in the recognition by all believers that they have been claimed by Christ precisely for the purpose of becoming his witnesses. The imperative of evangelism lies in the deeds of God which are its message, and its inevitability lies in the fact that they who evangelize are those who have been grasped by God's action, and know that their witness in word, deed, and oneness is the reflex of their faith-relation to their Lord. The love of Christ constrains them.[31]

Believing that God has made known in Jesus Christ the mystery of his will to save all [persons], we affirm that Christians are bound to confront [people] with the decision to commit themselves to him. We are required to make clear that this decision is a matter of life or death, that the call of the gospel is to full and abundant life here and now, and that those who decide for or against Jesus are not the same as they were prior to this decision.

The Lordship of Christ requires Christians to bear witness in matters of social structure. . . . In general, this witness is made through the very existence of the Christian community, and by its approving, questioning or challenging the patterns and practices of society around it, as well as by involvement of Christians in social responsibility.

In the missionary message itself, the Lordship of Christ over social structures and social change must be clearly proclaimed, as also this inescapable social obligation of Christian discipleship. In the contemporary world, political, social, economic and racial affairs play such a dominant part in the lives of people that the relevance of the gospel to human life must be demonstrated in these spheres.[32]

My own denomination, the former United Presbyterian Church in the United States of America, which as the result of the reunion with the Presbyterian Church in the United States is now the Presbyterian Church (U.S.A.), has been stressing evangelism for years. At its last meeting before the Reunion in June of 1983, the General Assembly adopted a resolution declaring evangelism to be "a necessary, urgent and major priority of the church." The action reiterated the statements of previous General Assemblies, including the 189th (1977), which adopted a report affirming its belief "that God's saving love in Jesus Christ includes all people. The United Presbyterian Church in the United States of America shares with all other churches the awesome yet joyful responsibility of sharing that good news in word and deed with all persons." The 196th General Assembly (1984) also approved a strong evangelism report.

Other denominations have made similar pronouncements affirming the importance and urgency of evangelism. So has the Roman Catholic Church. With a virtually universal mandate from the church, not to mention the biblical mandate, a local congregation cannot with impunity ignore its evangelistic responsibility. And there is still another mandate!

The World's Mandate

This is a different kind of mandate, which is laid upon us not as a command from the world but by the concern of our Christian conscience for the world. It is the mandate of need, which appeals to our basic Christian instincts. There is not only the Great Commission; there is also the Great Commandment to love God with all our heart, mind, soul, and strength and to express our love of God by loving our neighbors (Matt. 22: 37–38; Mark 12:30–31; Luke 10:27). Jesus makes it abundantly clear what the relationship is between our love of God and our love of neighbor in his hard-hitting parable of the separation of the sheep and the goats:

Then the righteous will answer him, "Lord, when did we see thee hungry and feed thee, or thirsty and give thee drink? And when did we see thee a stranger and welcome thee, or naked and clothe thee? And when did we see thee sick or in prison and visit thee?" And the King will answer them, "Truly, I say to you, as you did it to one of the least of these my brethren, you did it to me." Then he will say to those at his left hand, "Depart from me, you cursed, into the eternal fire prepared for the devil and his angels; for I was hungry and you gave me no food, I was thirsty and you gave me no drink, I was a stranger and you did not welcome me, naked and you did not clothe me, sick and in prison and you did not visit me." Then they also will answer, "Lord, when did we see thee hungry or thirsty or a stranger or naked or sick or in prison, and did not minister to thee?" Then he will answer them, "Truly, I say to you, as you did it not to one of the least of these, you did it not to me" (Matthew 25:37–45).

But of course there is always our human tendency to rationalize our failures and to justify our neglect. As an object lesson, take the lawyer's response to Jesus, after Jesus had commended him for reciting the Great Commandment. " 'You have answered right,' said Jesus; 'do this, and you will live.' But he, desiring to justify himself, said to Jesus, 'And who is my neighbor?' " How like that lawyer we are! When we're not doing what we ought to be doing, we try to justify ourselves by raising some intellectual smokescreen. We would rather debate about who our neighbors are than help them.

The lawyer's question occasioned one of Jesus' greatest parables, in which he confuted both the question and the attitude that prompted it (Luke 10:29–37). The point of the parable of the Good Samaritan is not Who is my neighbor? but To whom should I be a neighbor? And the answer is, To whoever needs me, including those who are not "my kind of people." The lawyer got the message. "Which of these three, do you think, proved neighbor to the man who fell among the robbers?" asked Jesus. "The one who showed mercy on him," replied the lawyer. And Jesus said to him, "Go and do likewise." That, too, is a mandate for us, for there is a hungry, hurting world about us. It calls for an evangelism motivated not by self-interest but by genuine compassion and love for our neighbors. It demands that we stretch our vision to see the whole world as our neighborhood, and those who are homeless or hungry, those who are victims of injustice, discrimination, or oppression of any kind, those whose basic human rights are denied, those who are suffering from poverty, disease, natural disaster, or deprivation or from any form of barbarity, brutality, or violence are those to whom we must be neighbors. It requires an evangelism that is sensitive to the kind of world in which we live, a world of desperate need.[33]

There is also what might be called the mandate of meaning. "What function is religion performing," asks Dean Kelley, "that is as essential to humankind as a carburetor is to an automobile? There are almost as many answers to this question as there are sociologists of religion, but most of their answers can be subsumed under a broad heading of which they are each special cases. What religion is 'doing' in every instance (albeit with greater or lesser effectiveness) is *explaining the meaning of life in ultimate terms.*"[34] The indispensable function of religion, according to Kelley, is to answer humanity's quest for meaning. Since religion cannot survive without institutions, religious organizations are the necessary conveyors of meaning, its embodiment as well as its carriers. "This suggests a different measure of success among religious groups. Those are successful which are explaining life to their members so that it makes sense to them."[35]

The quest for meaning is evident throughout the Bible, whether in Job's agonizing "Why did I not die at birth?" (Job 3:11), or the psalmist's wondering "What is man that thou art mindful of him?" (Ps. 8:4), or Jeremiah's lamenting "Why dost thou so long forsake us?" (Lam. 5:20), or the people's saying to one another at Pentecost, "What does this mean?" (Acts 2:12), or the disciples' asking Jesus about the signs of the times (Luke 21:7; Mark 13:4; Matt. 24:3). Our evangelism must speak to this fundamental quest for meaning, offering not easy solutions and cheap grace but the profound truth that without God there is no ultimate meaning, for what hope is there for the future of this planet if the future is not in God's hands? The Christian gospel has answers to the essential questions that have haunted humanity from the beginning—Where have I come from? Why am I here? What will happen to me when I die?—answers that speak to the heart of faith. To those who wonder about the finality of death, Jesus' offer of eternal life is good news indeed. To those who are fearful of their own worthiness to stand before a righteous God, Jesus' promise of forgiveness is incredibly good news. To be liberated, not from dying but from the fear of death, is to know a freedom that the unbelieving world does not know or understand. To be released by the sacrifice of Christ, not from our capacity to sin but from the burden of our guilt, is to experience a freedom that makes possible a new life in Christ, the abundant life that he taught and represented. His was a life lived for others, and so should ours be. Such a life is meaningfull life.

There is still another aspect of the world's mandate that should be mentioned. It is the mandate of survival. We earthlings are living under the very real threat of annihilation. A Martian viewing our shenanigans would have to be thoroughly disgusted with the stupidity of the human race. The madness of the nuclear arms race; the rapacious abuse, misuse, and waste of the earth's natural resources; the pollution of the land, the sea, and the air; the elimination and endangering of more and more species of wildlife; the increase in the number of people suffering from hunger, poverty, and disease; the myopic selfishness and greed of persons and of nations, of classes and of races, the age-old struggle of the "haves" denying and discriminating against the "have-nots" and the "have-nots" struggling to become "haves"; the creeping corrosion of public and personal morality reflected in business, politics, and entertainment, the drug culture, the "me" generation, and the violence, terrorism, crime, and corruption that the inhabitants of this planet inflict upon each other daily—all are a manifestation of human sin and monstrous proof that the world needs a Savior. The world needs Jesus Christ!

We must, therefore, proclaim and demonstrate a gospel relevant for such a world, not an obscurantist gospel that invites people to withdraw from the world but one that challenges them to live in the world as Christ's representatives. The people to whom our Lord sends us must hear the demands as well as the promises of the gospel, and the church as evangelist must address the social evils as well as the personal sins of its time, the corporate structures and systems that enslave and dehumanize people as well as the individuals responsible. As Christians we ought to be encouraging people by our words and deeds to work together for the common good instead of striving separately for our own good. If our gospel does not offer the hope of peace and goodwill on earth, it can hardly be called good news. Would that the nations would invest as much in peacemaking as they do in the weapons of war. It is a matter of survival.

That is the mandate the world lays upon us, a mandate of need, of meaning, and of survival. What, then, is the content of the gospel we proclaim to the world?

THE MESSAGE

The indispensable need for a relevant gospel has been underscored throughout this chapter. A few words need to be said about the specific content of the message. To be sure, the application should vary according to the situation. There is, however, a core of truth that does not vary, for the heart of the gospel is Jesus Christ, "the same yesterday and today and for ever" (Heb. 13:8). Jesus Christ is the good news, and the good news is Jesus Christ. There is only one gospel, but each person incorporates and applies that gospel according to a personal faith commitment and understanding. So Paul could use the expression "according to my gospel" (Rom. 2:16, 16:25), yet admonish the Galatians for turning to a different gospel "—not that there is another gospel, but there are some who trouble you and want to pervert the gospel of Christ" (Gal. 1:6–7). The task of the evangelist is to make *the* gospel his or her gospel so that others will embrace it as their gospel. To be faithful to the message so that the message is relevant to the situation: that is the evangelistic challenge. Jesus Christ is the good news, but why and how is he good news for today?

The sad truth of the matter is that many people never hear

the gospel—even in church! At every lay people's seminar or
workshop I have ever conducted, someone inevitably makes a
comment to that effect. Such a comment evoked from one frustrated pastor the retort, "My congregation wouldn't know it if
they heard it!" He might have needed an outlet for his indigna-
tion, but what he said was wrong. Not all people but some
people will always know the gospel when they hear it. And some
will respond.

But not too many lay men and women (and not all pastors,
I might add) feel themselves capable of presenting the gospel to
someone else. They might find John Stott's exposition of the
gospel very helpful.[36] There are at least five elements, which
Stott identifies as follows:

1. The gospel events. These, of course, are the story of Jesus:
his birth, life, death, resurrection, and ascension. The Christian
witness should know the story. In their preaching and teaching,
Peter and Paul focused on Jesus' death and resurrection, presenting them not merely as historical but as saving events.
"Christ died for our sins" (1 Cor. 15:3) and was "raised for our
justification" (Rom. 4:25).

2. The gospel witnesses. By witnesses Stott means the evidence to which the apostles appealed to authenticate the gospel,
including the scriptures (the Old Testament) and their own eyes.
So Paul pointed out to the Corinthians that what had happened
to Jesus was "in accordance with the scriptures" (2 Cor. 15:3),
and Peter quoted the scriptures in his sermon at Pentecost. The
scriptures lent authority to the apostles' words. The events were
the fulfillment of the scriptures. But they also could speak with
the authority of their own experience. "This Jesus God raised
up, and of that we all are witnesses," declared Peter (Acts 2:32).
Paul, in enumerating the postresurrection appearances of Jesus,
commented that "he appeared to more than five hundred brethren at one time, most of whom are still alive." In other words,
they could substantiate Paul's story, or, what was even more
impressive, they could have refuted it, if what Paul was saying
were not true. And then there are the opening words of 1 John:
"That which was from the beginning, which we have heard,
which we have seen with our eyes, which we have looked upon

and touched with our hands, concerning the word of life—the life was made manifest, and we saw it, and testify to it" (1:1–2). There is yet another witness Stott could have mentioned, the Holy Spirit, as Jesus himself said, "But when the Counselor comes, whom I shall send to you from the Father, even the Spirit of truth, who proceeds from the Father, he will bear witness to me" (John 15:26). Again quoting Peter, "And we are witnesses to these things, and so is the Holy Spirit whom God has given to those who obey him" (Acts 5:32).

3. The gospel affirmations. Jesus is Lord (Rom. 10:9) and Jesus is Savior (1 John 4:14); "no one can say 'Jesus is Lord' except by the Holy Spirit" (1 Cor. 12:3). As Stott observes, the doctrine of the incarnation and the doctrine of the atonement are unique to Christianity. The descents or incarnations of Hinduism are unhistorical, incidental, and frequent. Christ's was once for all. The promise of forgiveness by a merciful Allah in Islam is made to those who are meritorious, according to how their merits are weighed on Allah's scales. Jesus Christ died for sinners. The symbol of the gospel is the cross, not the scales.

4. The gospel promises. Stott mentions two: the forgiveness of sins and the gift of the Holy Spirit. The gospel is not just what Christ did but what he now offers. Forgiveness is the essential ingredient of salvation (Luke 24:47; Acts 2:38, 10:43, 13:38–39). The promise is that if we repent of our sins and believe in Christ, we will be forgiven. Jesus also promised the gift of the Holy Spirit: "I will pray the Father, and he will give you another Counselor, to be with you for ever, even the Spirit of truth. . . . These things I have spoken to you, while I am still with you. But the Counselor, the Holy Spirit, whom the Father will send in my name, he will teach you all things, and bring to your remembrance all that I have said to you" (John 14:16–17, 25–26). The Holy Spirit is the source of the new life in Christ and the assurance of eternal life.

5. The gospel demands. The two requirements of the gospel, under which Stott includes some implications that could be listed as separate demands, are repentance and baptism (Acts 2:38). Repentance involves a complete turnaround *(metanoia)*, a change of mind and heart. The Greek word implies much

more than a verbal confession of one's sins; it denotes a turning
from sin, with a view to amending one's ways. Along with that
is the acceptance of Jesus Christ as Lord and Savior and the
commitment of one's life to him. Believing in Christ could be
given equal billing as a specific requirement. Either way, it is the
sine qua non of the gospel. The other demand is baptism, which
unites the believer to the body of Christ. I applaud Stott for
asserting very plainly that there is no conversion without church
membership. Nor can there be a conversion to God without a
conversion to one's neighbor. "Thus social responsibility
becomes an aspect not of Christian mission only, but also of
Christian conversion."[37] Commitment to one's neighbor is concomitant to accepting the Christ as Lord.

Although such a division of elements is unavoidably arbitrary
and artificial, I find Stott's anatomy of the gospel a very helpful
teaching aid. It seems to give lay people the handles they need
to grasp the total concept. It is also a useful evangelistic tool,
as people can be taught to stress the particular element that
seems most relevant to the existential situation. If, for example,
a person is feeling the burden of guilt, the promises of the gospel
are good news indeed. On the other hand, someone who is
looking for cheap grace may need to hear the demands of the
gospel.

The good news about Jesus is that he died for our sins, was
raised, and now reigns as Lord and Savior, with authority to
forgive sins and to bestow the Holy Spirit on those who believe,
all in accordance with the scriptures. This, says Stott, is what
is meant by proclaiming the kingdom of God, whose rule is now
exercised by Christ.

It is essential for the pastor-evangelist to remember that the
kingdom of God was the central theme of Jesus' preaching and
teaching. "Jesus came into Galilee, preaching the gospel of God,
and saying, 'The time is fulfilled, and the kingdom of God is at
hand; repent, and believe in the gospel' " (Mark 1:14–15; cf.
Matt. 4:17). The kingdom of God is the rule of God, or "God
ruling." The parables of Jesus reveal the paradoxical nature of
the kingdom, which is both present and future, realized and yet
to come, fulfilled in Christ but not consummated, something

God gives but which can be refused or missed. It is both the reign of God and the realm of God. The kingdom is God's, not ours; God's to build and God's to give. Its signs are the words and works of Jesus, and to accept or reject Jesus is to accept or reject the kingdom.

If the message of evangelism has an appropriate kingdom emphasis, it will be Trinitarian in its expression and church-related in its orientation. The fact that the kingdom is the rule of God is the basis and the thrust of the social gospel. "The distinctive ethical principles of Jesus were the direct outgrowth of his conception of the kingdom of God," wrote Walter Rauschenbusch, whose name is so closely linked to the social gospel.[38] Rauschenbusch pointed out that the kingdom ideal provides a corrective for the influence of the church and the revolutionary force of Christianity. It is not merely ethical but has a rightful place in theology. "This doctrine is absolutely necessary to establish that organic union between religion and morality, between theology and ethics, which is one of the characteristics of the Christian religion. . . . The first step to the reform of the churches is the restoration of the doctrine of the kingdom of God."[39] The message of evangelism, therefore, must include the good news of the kingdom, in the manner of him whom to know as Savior and serve as Lord is the way to the kingdom, the truth of the kingdom, and the life in the kingdom.

This chapter has addressed some of the questions and concerns that pastors have about evangelism. It is important for the reader of a book like this to know where the author stands theologically, before seeing what one has to say about any kind of ministry. My intention was not to present an exhaustive treatment of the meaning and method of evangelism or of the mandate for evangelism, but rather to establish a theoretical base for what follows. My hope is that the more practical chapters will therefore have integrity as well as credibility with pastors who want to take seriously their role as evangelist.

3
The Pastor's Evangelistic Responsibility

It is entirely possible that we could have a clear understanding of evangelism, and even acknowledge the urgency of the task, without applying that understanding to ourselves as pastors. We could understand the meaning, accept the mandate, and affirm the message of evangelism without accepting our own responsibility to be evangelists. In other words, believing that evangelism is a good thing for the church, we accept the mandate for someone else ("those who are uniquely qualified for the role"), but not for ourselves. We affirm the message as central to our preaching, but that is as far as our evangelistic responsibility extends. I know pastors who feel this way. They believe evangelism is a specialized ministry for gifted individuals; it is not something they feel obligated to do or feel guilty for not doing. They are neither involved nor interested, and in too many cases they are even antagonistic about it, as my surveys have indicated. The issue is one we need to address.

SHOULD THE PASTOR BE AN EVANGELIST?

My answer is explicit in the Preface, as well as implicit throughout the first two chapters. I wish to address this question again, however, from a different perspective, not from that of the pastor's leadership role[40] but from the standpoint of the practice of ministry. Should the pastor be thinking evangelistically all the time? Some of the time? Any of the time? Is it appropriate for a pastor to be an evangelist when he or she is counseling, for example, or is that a betrayal of one's counseling role, as some have commented to me? Does being an evangelist destroy a pastor's objectivity and interject an ulterior motive into his or her relationships with unchurched persons?

These are legitimate concerns, which need to be taken seriously. Most pastors would admit there are occasions when it is appropriate to be evangelistic. Even the most adamant objectors to the role of pastor-evangelist have to admit, when pinned down, that there are times when a pastor must do the work of an evangelist. If so, then it is fair to say that the pastor, at least in some sense, should be an evangelist. But in what sense? That is the key question!

WHAT KIND OF PASTOR-EVANGELIST?

"Evangelist" is not an office the pastor holds, such as being Head of Staff, Moderator of the Session, President of the Corporation, or Chair of the Board of Deacons. It is not even a functional distinction that belongs uniquely to the pastor. It is rather a matter of perspective and of style. It is a way of relating to people, a concept of how one fulfills one's various roles as pastor. Far from detracting from the pastor's fulfillment of those roles, it should actually enhance his or her effectiveness as a preacher, teacher, worship leader, counselor, caller, administrator, equipper, and whatever other roles a pastor might have. It is true that an overzealous desire to convert a lost soul could sidetrack one's pastoral relationships, if allowed to do so. But that does not have to happen, nor is it at all what is intended to happen. Our desire is to turn people on, not off. If they are always tuning us out instead of in, we had better take a look at our style of evangelism.

We can learn much from the apostle Paul about the kind of evangelism we should teach and practice. He was not ashamed of the gospel (Rom. 1:16). He knew its power was in the cross of Christ, not in his own eloquence or wisdom (1 Cor. 1:17), and he resolved "to know nothing among you except Jesus Christ and him crucified" (1 Cor. 2:2). He acknowledged his own weaknesses and fears, in order that his hearers' faith "might not rest in the wisdom of [persons] but in the power of God" (1 Cor. 2:5). He identified with his hearers and tried to relate to them at their level of understanding and need, without compromising his message. Thus, when he addressed the men of Athens on the Areopagus, he began by commending them for being very religious, making reference to their objects of worship and using their altar "to an unknown god" as a contact point for proclaiming the gospel (Acts 17:22–31). He was direct but sensitive, attempting to be "all things to all [people], that I might by all means save some. I do it all for the sake of the gospel" (1 Cor. 9:22–23). He gave his personal testimony when it was appropriate to do so, as when he was before Felix the governor (Acts 24) and before Festus and Agrippa (Acts 26), and he proclaimed the gospel when proclamation was called for, as in the synagogues at Thessalonica and Beroea (Acts 17) and at Ephesus (Acts 19).

Through it all, Paul recognized his own inadequacy and his dependence upon God: "Not that we are sufficient of ourselves to claim anything as coming from us: our sufficiency is from God, who has qualified us to be ministers of a new covenant" (2 Cor. 3:5–6, adapted). Yet because his strength was in God and not in himself, he knew he was "sufficient for these things. For we are not, like so many, peddlers of God's word; but as [persons] of sincerity, as commissioned by God, in the sight of God, we speak in Christ" (2 Cor. 2:16–17). Paul's evangelistic integrity did not allow him to ignore or condone error or falsehood for fear of offending someone. Thus he blasted Elymas for seeking to turn away Sergius Paulus, the proconsul, from the faith: "You son of the devil, you enemy of all righteousness, full of all deceit and villainy, will you not stop making crooked the straight paths of the Lord?" (Acts 13:10). Paul also ministered to people's physical needs, as when he healed the father of Publius and other residents of the island of Malta (Acts 28:7–10).

Paul's personal ministry of evangelism continued even during his imprisonment in Rome, where people came to him in great numbers. "And he expounded the matter to them from morning till evening, testifying to the kingdom of God and trying to convince them about Jesus both from the law of Moses and from the prophets. And some were convinced by what he said, while others disbelieved" (Acts 28:23–24). From this last passage we see that Paul worked at it all day long, that he testified to the kingdom of God, with the scriptures as his authority, and that the results of his efforts were mixed. Some believed and some did not.

So, too, we could learn from studying the evangelistic styles of Peter and others in their personal encounters with different kinds of people in varying situations. We notice that they too ministered to human needs, as when Peter and John healed the lame beggar at the temple gate (Acts 3:1–10). Ananias healed Saul of his blindness (Acts 9:10–19), and Philip healed many who were lame or paralyzed in a city of Samaria (Acts 8:7). There are many examples of person-to-person evangelism in the New Testament, in which we see the disciples' characteristic directness, as with Peter in his confrontation of Simon the magician (Acts 8:14–24); their evangelistic teaching, as with Philip with the Ethiopian eunuch (Acts 8:26–39) and Paul and Silas with Lydia and her friends (Acts 16:13–15) and with the Philippian jailer and his family (Acts 16:23–34); their emphasis on repentance and baptism, as seen in Peter's witness to Cornelius and his household (Acts 10); and their dependence upon the Holy Spirit (Acts 8:29, 11:12, 13:9, and 16:18).

Peter's call to bear witness to Cornelius and Paul's missionary labors exemplify, of course, God's intention that the gospel be shared with all people, Jews and Gentiles alike, although there were the Judaizers (the circumcision party), who insisted on making the Gentiles in effect become Jews before they could become Christians: that is, "like us"! They even intimidated Peter into thinking that way, much to the consternation of Paul, who had to confront Peter about it (Gal. 2:11–14). And the establishment of churches throughout the Roman Empire reflects the corporate nature of their evangelism, the intention of which was to bring people into a community of believers, whose faith and understanding would be nurtured by their shared experiences of worship, study, fellowship, and service.

Although Jesus' evangelism was qualitatively and uniquely different from that of his disciples, we can learn much from the way he related to people. It is immediately evident that he ministered first to people's physical needs.[41] His approach was the quintessence of service evangelism. He related to people where they were, as they were, while seeing what they could be and holding up to them the possibilities of a new and better life. He invited, but he did not insist. He challenged, but he did not coerce. He condemned sin, yet he did not condemn the repentant sinner (John 8:1–11). But he did not mince words in confronting the hypocrisy of the Pharisees and the scribes (Matt. 23:1–36; Mark 12:38–40; Luke 20:46–47).

Jesus' evangelism, then, related to people at their point of need. His was a gospel of works as well as of words. He commissioned the seventy to "heal the sick, raise the dead, cleanse lepers, cast out demons" (Matt. 10:8). When they entered a town, they were to "heal the sick in it and say to them, 'The kingdom of God has come near to you' " (Luke 10:9). Thus their ministry was a sign of the kingdom. He exhorted people, if they could not believe that he and the Father were one, to believe in him because of the works he did (John 14:11), and he promised that those who believed in him "will also do the works that I do; and greater works than these will [they] do, because I go to the Father" (John 14:12). The gospel of Jesus Christ is a gospel of works: not of works righteousness but of righteous works, not the works of self-righteousness but the works of love. "A new commandment I give to you," he told the disciples, "that you love one another; even as I have loved you, that you also love one another. By this [everyone] will know that you are my disciples, if you have love for one another" (John 13:34–35; cf. 15:12–13).

Another pertinent word of Jesus was his test for determining true or false prophets. "You will know them," he declared, "by their fruits. Are grapes gathered from thorns, or figs from thistles? So, every sound tree bears good fruit, but the bad tree bears evil fruit. A sound tree cannot bear evil fruit, nor can a bad tree bear good fruit. . . . Thus you will know them by their fruits" (Matt. 7:16–20). The fruit test applies to modern prophets as well. Our application of the gospel to the issues of our times should be backed by the integrity of our own lives. The test of our authority is our loyalty to the gospel of Jesus Christ.

Thus there are evangelists and evangelists. The validity of a pastor's evangelistic ministry rests entirely upon the kind of evangelism she or he represents. True evangelism is inspired by God and informed by the examples of Jesus and the apostles. Let Paul's exhortation to his young protégé Timothy be his charge to us as well: "As for you, always be steady, endure suffering, *do the work of an evangelist,* fulfil your ministry" (2 Tim. 4:5, emphasis added).

WHAT ARE THE OBSTACLES?

We know many pastors are not doing the work of an evangelist. What are the barriers that prevent or discourage a minister from being a pastor-evangelist? There are some reasons why a pastor might not *want* to do evangelism, and some reasons why a pastor might not be *able* to do evangelism. The two realities are related, but the distinction should be kept in mind. I have arbitrarily grouped under several different categories a number of factors that could be viewed as hindrances to a pastor's ministry of evangelism.

Rational, Intellectual, Theological Barriers

Barriers in this group could include a distorted (negative) image of what evangelism is, or what a pastor-evangelist is, or what evangelists in general are, the last being formed by observations of self-styled "TV evangelists." Or there could be a genuine conviction, rationally conceived, that evangelism is not everyone's responsibility, or gift, or special calling. If one does not feel called to it or equipped to do it, one has no obligation to be a pastor-evangelist, so the thinking goes.

At the opposite extreme is the not infrequently held opinion that everything one does as a pastor is ipso facto evangelism. The deterrent to evangelism in such a stance is that if I am an evangelist by virtue of my pastoral calling, I probably will not give any thought to *being* an evangelist. If everything is evangelism, then nothing is evangelism. That conclusion has been verified over and over again for me, as I have observed the ministries of those who hold such an opinion. What happens almost without fail is that their being a pastor becomes their excuse for not being an evangelist!

Professional Barriers

Under this category I would include those barriers having to do mainly with professional skills. Some pastors have never had any training in evangelism. They never took a course in it at seminary, nor have they attended any kind of evangelism workshop or seminar. It is not that they are opposed to doing it; they just don't know how. They feel inadequate, and their sense of inadequacy keeps them from making any conscious efforts. They need to understand that much of what they do as pastors is, in fact, evangelism. Their problem is just the opposite of those referred to above, who think everything is evangelism.

Another obstacle to the pastor's evangelistic role, which I have categorized as a professional barrier but which could just as properly be listed as a theological barrier, has to do with both a style and a theology of ministry. Some pastors lay great stress, and rightly so, on the ministry of the *laos*. They believe their role and responsibility is to equip others to do the work of an evangelist, rather than their doing it. Whether that is another rationalization or a sincere theological conviction, it is unfortunate if that belief becomes a barrier to their own involvement. The issue is not whether evangelism should be done by pastors or lay people. Both should be involved. It is another both/and, not an either/or situation.

Personal Barriers

These include problems of personality and temperament. Some pastors, surprisingly enough, are not "people persons." Goodness knows how they ended up in the pastoral ministry, but they did, and the fact that they are not other-oriented is a real barrier to evangelistic effectiveness. It has nothing to do with being an extrovert or having an outgoing personality. It has to do with being a genuinely caring person, a good listener, someone to whom others relate easily and well. People who lack those qualities are not likely to be good evangelists.

Then, too, some people's temperament may be such that they lack the patience a pastor-evangelist should have. They may be too argumentative or judgmental, or even angry, when they don't intend to be. Their appearance may intimidate others, or make them feel uncomfortable, and sensing that, they conclude that person-to-person situations, including personal evangelism, are not their "bag."

Still another barrier under the above heading has to do with one's personal faith. Many a pastor has asked herself or himself, Do I really believe in a personal God? Do I really mean what I say in the pulpit? The pastor's personal faith is such an important factor that we shall discuss it more thoroughly in the next chapter.

Emotional and Psychological Barriers

As we have seen in our sample of pastors' concerns (Appendix A), pastors can have the same hang-ups with evangelism as anyone else. Fear of rejection can make a Clem Kadiddlehopper out of many a pastor. (Clem was Red Skelton's characterization of a timid salesman, who used to knock on doors and say, "Nobody home, I hope, I hope, I hope, I hope!") You will recall that some pastors in our sample were worried about imposing their views on others or about intruding. These are very real concerns. Failure is another fear that can be an obstacle to evangelism. Some people don't believe in the adage, "It is better to have loved and lost than never to have loved at all." Other pastors may be worried about their image. They do not want to be put into the same camp as other evangelists of whom they do not approve at all. Fear of ridicule or criticism can be a very large barrier.

So is the sheer terror of going one-on-one with another human being in somebody's living room, without the protection of a pulpit and the security of one's professional turf. Preaching belongs in the pulpit, not in the living room. Knowing that, some preachers feel totally out of their element when the situation calls for an interpersonal witness. They are too used to pontificating.

These are some of the barriers that keep pastors from doing the work of an evangelist. The reader will undoubtedly think of others, all of which add up to one basic question: How strong is my own faith? If I really believe the gospel, I can hardly refuse to share it with others. What is at stake here is the pastor's personal faith, and to that we now must turn.

4

The Pastor's Personal Faith

Of one thing I am certain: The sine qua non for evangelism is the personal faith of the evangelist. If one does not have one's own faith house in order, one is not at all likely to want to do evangelism. You can't share your faith if you don't have a faith to share. That applies to pastors as well as to everyone else.

My belief in the indispensability of faith does not mean the evangelist or witness can have no doubts. Faith and doubt are inseparable companions. An ordered faith house is not one swept clean of doubts and questions. Rather, it is one whose tenant knows the Landlord personally, even though the tenant is not always sure where the Landlord is, or what the Landlord wants, or why the Landlord doesn't seem to take care of some of the problems around the house. It is not necessary to have all the answers. It *is* crucial to know *that* one believes, *what* one believes, and *why* one believes.

Nor does my belief in the essentiality of faith preclude the possibility that some people bear witness falsely or hypocritically. Faith is essential for a sincere witness, not for an inauthentic one. Our words must have the ring of genuine conviction. It is hard to be convincing about a Savior we don't know personally. We might evoke the same reaction that the seven Jewish exorcists did when they pronounced the name of Jesus "over those who had evil spirits, saying, 'I adjure you by the Jesus whom Paul preaches.' . . . But the evil spirit answered them, 'Jesus I know, and Paul I know; but who are you?' " (Acts 19:13–15).

Christian faith *(pistis)* is centered on Jesus Christ, who is both its subject and its object, its pioneer and its perfecter (Heb. 12:2).

Faith in Christ involves a trust relationship. It is more than mere mental assent to his claims about himself. It is a total commitment of one's life to Christ, calling for belief in him as Savior and obedience to him as Lord. Faith in Christ illumines and edifies the Christian's faith in God. Christology informs theology. At least that is the way it worked for me. My faith in God preceded my faith in Christ. I believed in a personal God before I understood the meaning of or experienced a personal relationship with Christ. I cannot pinpoint the moment of initial awareness. It was and continues to be a gradual process, with plenty of ups and downs along the way. But now I have an inkling at least of what Paul meant when he said, "For to me to live is Christ" (Phil. 1:21). Now my understanding of God is informed by what Jesus taught about him by word and by example. If one wants to know what God is like, one has only to look at and listen to Jesus, who shows us what God expects of us, what God can do for us, and what God has already done for us.

I suspect that my faith pilgrimage is not unique. There are many people out there who say they believe in God but who do not know Jesus Christ. Their God-consciousness is a plug-in point for the Christian witness, who can have a deep faith-sharing experience with such persons. But in order to do so, the witness or evangelist must himself or herself be a person of faith, one who can talk about a God he or she knows personally. In that sense the pastor is truly God's man or God's woman.

THE IMPORTANCE OF FAITH

There are many ways of expressing the essential nature of personal faith. Let me suggest three main reasons why I think it is important for the pastor to be a person of faith.

A Matter of Power

First of all, it is a matter of power. Remember Jesus' words to his disciples just before his ascension. "You shall receive power when the Holy Spirit has come upon you; and you shall be my witnesses" (Acts 1:8). Note the order. First they would receive the gift of the Holy Spirit; then they would be his witnesses. In other words, we have to be empowered to witness. In Chapter 3 we noted the apostles' dependence upon the Holy Spirit in their missionary labors. It was Peter filled with the Holy Spirit whose boldness impressed the people he addressed in Jerusalem concerning the cripple he had healed (Acts 4: 8–12). It was Paul filled with the Holy Spirit who confronted Elymas the magician (Acts 13:8–9). It was Stephen full of the Holy Spirit who saw the vision of God and Jesus just before he was stoned to death (Acts 7:55). The evangelist's power must come from God, received by grace through faith. Jesus told his disciples that he was the vine and they were the branches. If they abided in him, they would bear much fruit; apart from him they could do nothing (John 15:5).

If such a relationship with the triune God is essential, it is obvious that the pastor's devotional life is of the utmost importance. At a recent seminar on "The Pastor as Person" I asked the group of ministers who were there to share what they were presently doing by way of personal devotions. The response was most impressive and encouraging, as one by one the pastors described their devotional life. Disciplined Bible study, regular prayer times, devotional reading, and meditation were consistent parts of their routines. All agreed that one's prayer life was a matter of self-discipline, and that like any other good habit one has to work at it. I liken it to using dental floss; it's easy to get out of the habit. The longer you go without doing it, the easier it becomes to find reasons for not doing it and for letting other things interfere.

That might not have been a typical group, for many pastors will admit that their devotional life is at best not what it ought to be and that at worst it has been largely if not completely neglected. The pressures and demands on most pastors are horrendous, with the result that their devotional life falls by the wayside. It is easy, furthermore, for pastors to rationalize their failure at this point, because of all the "spiritual" things they do professionally. Invocations at service clubs and church board meetings become substitutes for private prayer, and sermon preparation displaces devotional Bible reading. Some pastors come to regard their being asked to say grace at congregational dinners as an occupational hazard!

It is a tragedy when a pastor becomes a professional pray-er, who talks about God but never *to* God, who is informed about the Bible but not inspired by it, who preaches about the spiritual disciplines but doesn't practice them. Prayer is the pipeline to spiritual power. The current needs a conductor. The very fact that a pastor's life is so pressurized and hectic is all the more reason not for neglecting but for deepening one's devotional life. I know that I personally could not have survived the exigencies of a pastor's life without a strong faith in God, whose presence I felt, whose strength I depended upon, whose forgiveness I needed, and whose grace was always sufficient. I can identify completely with Paul, when he wrote that "the life I now live in the flesh I live by faith in the Son of God" (Gal. 2:20). It's a matter of power.

A Matter of Example

Paul enjoined Timothy to "set the believers an example in speech and conduct, in love, in *faith*, in purity" (1 Tim. 4:12, emphasis added). Some years ago there was a tendency to downplay the responsibility of the pastor to be an example to the flock. "We should be pointing to Christ, not to ourselves," was the argument used by those who felt that way. Its plausibility lends credence to the notion, which persists among many today who object to the double standard imposed upon ministers and to the pastor-on-the-pedestal syndrome. They have a point! The peril of denying one's responsibility to be an example, however, is that it can be an excuse to indulge whatever one wants to indulge. Some pastors are anxious to let other people know that pastors are only human. As if that isn't obvious! But some pastors don't want to be guilty, as they feel some of their professional counterparts are, of having a phobia about their public image. There *are* pastors who try to hide or deny their humanity. There is an immense difference, however, between admitting our humanity and flaunting it.

It is a fact of life that people do expect their pastor to be an example, whether we like it or not. We can object to that reality and complain about it, but we ignore it at our own risk. There are some things a pastor simply cannot do with impunity, and it is naive if not stupid to think otherwise. If we insist on letting our humanity hang out all over the place, we are going to have to pay the price. The question is not whether to be or not to be an example. We don't have that choice. We are examples, willy-nilly. The question is what kind of example are we going to be. An example is not a standard. An example points to something else. Christ is the standard. We exemplify not Christ but those who seek to follow him, those who know they need his forgiveness and whose confidence and strength are not in themselves but in Christ. So Paul could urge the Corinthians to "be imitators of me, as I am of Christ" (1 Cor. 11:1).

That theme is reflected in the ordination services of many denominations, as it is in the one for the ordination of elders in the Presbyterian *Book of Common Worship,* where the congregation is charged to "follow them so far as you see them follow Christ."[42] One of the ordination vows when I was ordained as a Presbyterian minister included the promise to walk "with *exemplary* piety before the flock."[43] The same idea is expressed in different words in the ordination service for ministers of the reunited Presbyterian Church (U.S.A.), when the congregation promises "to follow as he (she) guides us, serving Jesus Christ, who alone is Head of the church" and to "honor his (her) authority as he (she) seeks to honor and obey Jesus Christ our Lord."[44] Leadership is best exercised by example. Insofar as pastors are called to be leaders, they are called to be examples. People can be expected to honor the pastor's authority if the pastor seeks to honor Christ. To be an example is an inescapable implication and condition of good leadership.

So Paul appealed for self-control in all these, "lest after preaching to others I myself should be disqualified" (1 Cor. 9:27). It behooves a pastor, as he said to Timothy, to set the believers an example in faith, as well as in the other ways he mentioned. I happen to believe that what people want and need from us more than anything else is precisely that: an example of faith. They want to believe that we preachers really believe what we say, and they want to see evidence of it in our own lives. Nothing is more encouraging to one's faith, including my own, than the evidences of faith we see in those around us. Their faith strengthens my faith, and my faith strengthens their faith. If I really believe in a personal God, it should motivate, inform, condition, guide, judge, and redeem everything I do.

When faith is there, it is evident. But faith never shows when it's on display. It is not to be worn as a badge or a label. Faith is made manifest in the courage of one's convictions, in the boldness of one's stand for truth, in the spiritual quality of one's life. It shows in the confidence one has in the God who in everything is working for good with those who love him (Rom. 8:28). So when the elders and scribes "saw the boldness of Peter and John, and perceived that they were uneducated, common men, they wondered; and they recognized that they had been with Jesus" (Acts 4:13). And so Paul's boldness allowed him to offer himself as an example of faith. "Now you have observed my teaching, my conduct, my aim in life, my *faith,* my patience, my love, my steadfastness" (2 Tim. 3:10, emphasis added).

In short, if we are to be witnesses to our flocks and to the world, then we should be setting the believers an example of faith. How else can we expect them to obey the injunction of the writer of Hebrews: "Remember your leaders, those who spoke to you the word of God; consider the outcome of their life, and imitate their faith" (Heb. 13:7)?

A Matter of Integrity

It is, after all, a matter of personal integrity. How can I preach with integrity about a God I don't know personally? How can I bear witness to a Savior and Lord in whom I don't really believe? "I am not ashamed," declared Paul, "for I know whom I have believed, and I am sure that he is able to guard until that Day what has been entrusted to me" (2 Tim. 1:12). Here I must reveal something about my own faith struggle. I went through a period in my ministry when I felt a desperate need to know that what I said I believed was really true. It was prompted by my graduate studies in comparative religions, as I wrestled with the conflicting truth claims of other world religions, taught in many cases by adherents of those faiths. Is Christianity the true religion? Was Jesus "the only-begotten Son of God, begotten of the Father before all worlds, God of God, Light of Light, Very God of Very God," as the Nicene Creed affirms? How could I be sure? How could I know? I had to know, if I was going to keep on preaching. How else could I preach with integrity?

And what about the Bible? Was it really inspired by God? Is it the Word of God? If I believe that it is, *why* do I believe it? And do I without reservation believe it to be "the only infallible rule of faith and practice," as I vowed I did when I was ordained?[45] I had to answer these questions, and my answers would determine whether I could go on being a minister. I had to know *why* I believe and what I believe. It was and is a matter of integrity.

THE PARADOX OF FAITH

That necessity plunged me headlong into a deep probe of my own spirituality, in which the paramount issue for me was the paradoxical nature of faith. Pastors should be and are more aware than most people of that paradox. On the one hand, there is a sense in which the decision to believe or not to believe in God is entirely up to us. We have the freedom to accept or reject God. On the other hand, once we are believers, we realize that our decision was not our initiative but our response to God's prior love. God was seeking us, before we ever wanted him. Who better than a pastor should know that grace precedes faith? No matter how late in life it happens, when the call finally comes we understand what Isaiah meant when he spoke of being formed from the womb to be the Lord's servant (Isa. 49:5). God calls and uses even those who do not know him, as he did Cyrus, the king of Persia (Isa. 45:4). And as Paul reminded the Christians at Rome, "God shows his love for us in that while we were yet sinners Christ died for us" (Rom. 5:8). As long as we are struggling to believe, we think it all depends on us. Once we do believe, we know it all depends on God.

But we know that only after the fact. This is the tension of what I call the gift and the grasp. What prompts us to search for God? The urge to grasp is itself a gift! The gift-grasp relationship is contiguous, conterminous, and continuous. When they are coincident, that is faith! Most of us go on grasping for God as long as we live, for like Isaiah we may think at times, "Truly, thou art a God who hidest thyself" (Isa. 45:15). We depend upon God to renew our faith daily, and our prayer, like that of the psalmist, should be "Lord, take not thy holy Spirit from me" (Ps. 51:11).

Yet there are times when God is very near and very real to us, and it is those experiences of God's presence that confirm our faith. As a pastor-evangelist I wanted to be able to make a rational case for an experiential faith, so that I could preach, teach, evangelize, and bear witness with intellectual as well as spiritual integrity. The soul-searching process continues, but I now can say, after much reading, discussion, reflection, and prayer, that I know what I believe and why I believe it. That does not mean I have all the answers to my faith questions. It means that I know what the questions are and which ones I can or cannot answer. I am aware of the limitations and the risks of faith, as well as of its possibilities and rewards.

Most people have at least a vague idea of what they believe, but I have found that very few people know or have thought about *why* they believe what they believe. What I mean is, their reasons for believing in God are not real reasons. They confuse the *what* and the *why* of their faith. It's not that they don't have their "reasons." The trouble is that they don't realize that their "reasons" are not reasons for someone else to believe. Therein lies the problem for doing evangelism. Too many evangelists operate on assumptions not shared by their hearers. They have failed to recognize that their "reasons" are really faith statements, that their subjective affirmations of *what* they believe are not objective reasons *why* they believe. Their statements are conclusions, not reasons; assumptions, not proofs.

The evangelist or witness must recognize the difference between the *what* and the *why* of faith. The objective of telling the *what* is to be understood; the objective of answering the *why* is to be believable. The *what* should give clarity to the *why;* the *why* should give integrity to the *what.*

It is in fact impossible to say why we believe in God without using faith statements. Our reasons are always tautologies and purely subjective. It is not that our truth claims are not a valid expression of our belief. It is, rather, that they are not self-evident to a nonbeliever. The importance of this reality for doing evangelism cannot be gainsaid and must be understood. One's quest for an answer to the *why* of faith will lead to the inevitable conclusion that faith has to be a gift. "For by grace you have been saved through faith; and this is not of your own doing, it is the gift of God" (Eph. 2:8; cf. 1 Cor. 12:9, 4:7; 2 Tim. 1:6). Faith defers to grace. Faith acknowledges its own contingency, confesses its own limitations. My theologizing and intellectualizing led me to the conclusion, therefore, that the apparent antinomy of the gift and the grasp is only a pseudo paradox, for it finds its resolution in the grace of God.

THE IMPLICATIONS OF FAITH

If faith is ultimately God's gift, what are the implications for evangelism? Preaching? Interpersonal witnessing? The art of Christian persuasion? As I pointed out in the section on faith sharing (see Chapter 2), making a case for God becomes a matter of sharing those experiences which are for us the evidence that confirms our faith assumption. If the givenness of faith is taken seriously, it will have an enormous impact on our evangelistic style, for to acknowledge our dependence upon God for the very faith to believe in God leaves no room for arrogance and unbounded self-confidence. To accept the givenness of faith is to acknowledge that there is no way we can circumscribe God's omniscience, or circumvent God's omnipotence, or obviate God's initiative, or preempt God's freedom. Nor can we transcend our dependence upon God. We should not impose our temporality on God's eternality, or think that human discovery can usurp the place of divine revelation.

Awareness of the givenness of faith also paves the way for a mutual sharing with other persons, who are much less likely to be turned off or offended by a personal experience of God sensitively related, especially if the witness has been a good listener.

From all that has been said so far, there are also some important inferences to be drawn regarding the role of faith in the pastor's ministry of evangelism, the way one relates to people, and the way one understands oneself. The first is that if faith is a gift of God, then normal human beings should be able to have faith. Religious faith differs from other gifts in this regard. The gift of intellectual, mechanical, or artistic genius is given to some individuals and not to others. But not so the gift of faith. It is offered to all persons; otherwise, what would be the meaning of a decision of faith? That is, if it were not possible for anyone to respond to Christ, how could we be responsible for accepting the call of Jesus to follow him? The gift is offered to everyone. "For God so loved the world [that's everyone!] that he gave his only Son, that whoever [that's anyone!] believes in him should not perish but have eternal life" (John 3:16). Jesus came to save the whole world (John 12:47).

What about the instances in the Bible where God is said to have hardened the hearts of people, Pharaoh for instance (Ex. 4:21, 7:3, et al.)? Whatever that difficult concept means, it surely cannot mean that God is to be blamed for every instance of denial, betrayal, apostasy, and sin. The Bible affirms God's sovereignty and God's freedom to choose and to use whomever he will, however he will, to accomplish his purposes. In his permissive will, God hardens the hearts of those who resist and oppose him. We had best leave the arbitrariness of God's dealings with people as an unanswered question. Pharaoh's attitude must have been akin to the sin against the Holy Spirit, which Jesus said is unforgivable. Pharaoh refused to acknowledge the truth when Moses confronted him with it. It suited God's purpose to allow Pharaoh to follow his stubborn inclinations. But God has never refused anyone who is open and receptive to his will. So anyone can have the gift of faith.

But not everyone does have it! That is the second inference, which is confirmed by both experience and scripture. There was Pharaoh and there was Moses! It seems that some people have a greater capacity for faith than do others. They have what I call spiritual sensitivity, a capacity for relating and responding to other people in a Christlike way. I first became aware of this quality through the life of a child who was unusually gifted in this regard, more so than his brothers and sisters, who were normal, healthy children but who did not have the same degree of spiritual sensitivity. There was no way to account for it except to say that it was a gift of God, just as much as a high I.Q. or some other form of giftedness that society has long recognized.

But society has never looked upon spiritual sensitivity as a gift. That's too bad, for the world needs this gift. There are children who have it. They may not be sophisticated about religious matters, but they have a sensitivity for God. They reflect it in the prayers they offer, the questions they ask, the things they say, the way they relate to other children and to adults, and in the overall quality of their lives.

The same is true of some adults. There are those who have the same gift of spiritual sensitivity. They are godly people, though they may not be members of a church or even Christians. I have met persons of other faiths who are spiritually sensitive, godly people. I happen to be a Christian, and for me to live is Christ. My faith is wrapped up in him. My whole orientation is Christ-centered, and I think, speak, and act from a Christian point of view. Because I am a Christian, I am all the more ready to affirm truth wherever I find it, and there is much truth to be found in the scriptures of other religions. What is unique about Christianity is not the truth of its teachings. The uniqueness of Christianity is Jesus Christ! Christianity, as many have said, is Jesus Christ, and we who believe in him believe that we have been given a fuller revelation of God through him— sufficient for our salvation! If I did not believe that, I could not be a Christian. I believe Jesus Christ is the Savior of the world, and in that sense I believe Christianity is the true religion.[46]

But that is an affirmation of faith, and only those who have received the gift can say that. "No one can come to me," said Jesus, "unless the Father who sent me draws [that person]" (John 6:44, 65). That is another testimony to the givenness of faith. Only those who have received the gift know the truth of Jesus' words. If one does not know it, one has not received it!

And if one does not have it, then one probably will not recognize it in other people. In other words, it takes one to know one. Anyone who is not spiritually sensitive will be less likely to recognize the quality in someone else, or may mistake it for some other quality one admires in another person, but cannot identify with. In a word, not everyone has the gift of faith.

A third inference, therefore, is that faith should never be taken for granted. If faith is a gift of God, it is God's to give and God's to take away. If we can't make ourselves have it, we can't make ourselves keep it. We have all observed young people who were once close to God turn away from God in high school or college. What happened to them? Sometimes they go through a period of doubt or disbelief and come out of it with a stronger faith than they had before. Sometimes it works the other way, and they lose their faith entirely.

Or think of those individuals who make a beautiful profession of faith when they join the church, only to fall away a few months or years later. Why? Some say, "Well, they never really had it in the first place, or they wouldn't have lost it." I don't agree with that statement at all. It is simply not true that everyone who falls away from church "never had it in the first place." Some may not have, but many, if not most, did. They were as sincere as anyone else when they took their vows. Despite all the attempts to explain why some people become "apathetic and bored," as John Savage describes them, no one can explain why that happens to one person and not to another, both of whom were exposed to the same influences, good and bad. My point is that we cannot take the gift of faith for granted, our own faith or anyone else's.

That leads to a fourth inference, to which I have already alluded. If faith is a gift, it should never be a source of pride. I mean that overweening, self-righteous, pharisaical pride that Jesus so roundly condemned. Why are we human beings so prone to be conceited about our God-given gifts, as if we had acquired them by ourselves? To God and God alone belongs the credit for all our gifts, including the gift of faith. Paul put it squarely to the Corinthians when he asked, "What have you that you did not receive? If then you received it, why do you boast as if it were not a gift?" (1 Cor. 4:7). How could anyone say it better? Our confidence has to be in God, not in our own ability to have faith. Those who rely on their own ability to believe may be in for a big letdown. Through Christ we have confidence in God, as Peter reminds us, so that our faith and hope are in God, not in ourselves (1 Peter 1:21).

There is one more inference to be drawn from the givenness of faith, and that has to do with the obligations it imposes upon the recipients. To accept the implications of saying that faith is a gift of God is terribly threatening, because the demands it makes upon us are staggering. For if faith is a gift of God, we cannot bury it, or hoard it, or waste it, or neglect it. We cannot abuse it or misuse it. We must be stewards of the gift of faith, just as we are called to be stewards of all the other gifts of God. That means we are obligated to grow in our faith, to develop it, as Jesus' parable of the talents makes clear (Matt. 25:14–30). The moment we say "I believe!" is just the beginning. For the rest of our lives we clerics—like everyone else—must struggle with the problems, the challenges, the decisions, and the demands of faith. Understanding the word of God and interpreting it to our people is a challenge that demands our best intellect, our purest devotion, and our deepest dedication. We should be moving constantly from faith toward knowledge, not the other way around. Knowledge confirms what faith affirms. Like Peter, we should be able to say, "We have believed, and have come to know . . . " (John 6:69).[47] Too many pastors stop growing theologically when they leave seminary. They don't stretch themselves intellectually or spiritually, and their faith withers. If faith is a gift, we have to nourish it.

We are also obligated to share it. God's gifts are not meant for self-indulgence. Some pastors are averse to or afraid of sharing their faith experiences with their congregations. They have never talked about their relationship with Christ or invited people to share theirs. Board meetings are strictly business. Superficial home visits are baptized with a brief closing prayer. The pulpit is a screen from behind which they deliver their impersonal expositions or their scholarly dissertations or their brilliant commentaries on current events, but nothing about their faith struggles and victories or their commitment to a living Lord and Savior. How can they expect their people to understand what that relationship is like if it's never talked about? Why is that so hard for some pastors to do, some of the same ones who are willing to let the rest of their humanity hang out?

I say, if faith is a gift, we are obligated as servants of Christ and stewards of the mysteries of God (1 Cor. 4:1) to grow in our faith and to share it. But more than that, we are also obligated to *live* it, for as Paul states, we are "created in Christ Jesus for good works" (Eph. 2:10). James put it more bluntly: "Faith by itself, if it has no works, is dead" (James 2:17). Our good works, of course, should be the result of our faith, not the basis of it. Pastors know they are responsible to God. If they are men and women of faith, they know that God is very much involved in their life and work. They rely on God, and report to God, and represent God, because they know they are responsible to God. That is part of their obligation as stewards of the gift of faith.

The emphasis in this chapter has been on the givenness of faith. By no means is there any intention to minimize the reality of the grasp side of the paradox. The faith struggle goes on forever, even for those whose faith is strong. For faith is a ride on a roller coaster, for pastors as well as for everyone else. That very fact is not a liability but an asset to pastor-evangelists, for it enables us to relate more closely and easily to people, all of whom experience the same vicissitudes of faith. Maybe the reader can identify with my attempt to express this truth in one of my pulpit poems, entitled "Roller-Coaster Ride," written for use in a sermon I once preached on the ups and downs of faith:

Faith is a roller-coaster ride for clergy, clerks, or clowns.
The best disciples, old and new, have had their ups and downs.

The psalmist and the prophet had their moments of despair,
And even Jesus on the cross had doubts that God was there.

When faith is riding on the ridge, it shows in word and deed,
For mountains move if faith is but a grain of mustard seed.

It's not that we make miracles by *willing* to believe.
Faith's not a work, but God's free gift, that we by grace receive.

That thought should keep us humble, when we're feeling strong and
   tall.
The higher up the heights we climb, the farther we can fall!

For just as winter follows fall, and nighttime follows day,
We do not always sail the crest nor on the summit stay,

But sometimes plummet down the steeps with such breathtaking
   speed,
That roller-coaster riders should this warning hear—and heed!

Yet when the coaster car is at the bottom of the slope,
The peaks of faith loom large and give new impetus to hope.

Then we recall those moments when our faith in God was sure.
Confirmed by Truth, sustained by Love, we find we can endure

The ups and downs of faith. Indeed, we then can say,
Without the lows there'd be no highs, without the night, no day.

The ride is always risky, even scary, I'll agree.
But if we stay inside the car of faith, we're safe. You see,

The roller-coaster Maker is the one who takes the toll.
The car won't ever leave the track, if he is in control.

So *re* the roller-coaster ride, I'll take my own advice,
And hang on tight until the end, no matter what the price.

For when the ride is over, and the ups and downs are through,
I pray I'll be with God—and all the other riders, too!

5

The Pastor's Evangelistic Opportunities

Keeping in mind the obstacles that might deter or prevent a pastor from doing evangelism, or from being a vocal witness, we ask what opportunities a pastor has for evangelism. How does one identify opportunities? How can one learn to take advantage of those recognizable opportunities? Better yet, how can one create one's own opportunities for faith sharing? In this chapter we shall address these questions from the standpoint of the personal qualities required.

IDENTIFYING OPPORTUNITIES

We must admit that we do not always recognize our opportunities for an evangelistic witness, let alone avail ourselves of them. We rub shoulders every day with people with whom we could have a faith-sharing experience, or to whom we could present some aspect of the gospel that would help them, and we go on our way blissfully unaware of the golden opportunities we have missed. There are people all around us who need to hear the good news of Jesus Christ, but they don't hear it from us. People come to us for counseling, and the one thing we have to share that secular counselors do not is our faith in Jesus Christ, but how often does that inform our counseling? A clinical psychologist at the USAF Medical Center at Scott Air Force Base told a group of Air Force chaplains attending a pastoral ministry workshop a few years ago that too many clergy have displaced spirituality with psychology. He lamented the loss of the spiritual dimension in their everyday lives. "Most people," he said, "will seek out clergy for guidance in their marital disorders or personality conflicts before they will seek out a clinical psychologist, psychiatrist, or social worker. But you should be very discerning as to what psychological theories and practices you give yourselves over to, for many of them very clearly do not complement the spiritual, cannot be integrated into the spiritual, but actually displace the spiritual. . . . [Pastors] will not be able to offer spiritually what their congregations will be pleading for in the years to come."[48] Prophetic wisdom from a psychologist!

Then again, we clergy live in communities with neighbors who have no relationship with God, but we do nothing to help them find one. We serve on all sorts of civic, social, educational, and other community boards and committees, belong to organizations of all kinds, meet people at parties and other social gatherings in the neighborhood and elsewhere, have contact with those who deliver our mail, empty our trash, wait upon us in stores, cut or dress our hair, service our cars, teach our children, read our water meters, paint our houses, and serve us in countless other ways, but with how many of these people do we ever share our faith or invite them to share theirs? To identify the opportunities to do so we need evangelistic sensitivity, theological awareness, and a listening ear.

Evangelistic sensitivity. Sensitivity can be developed, if there is a conscious commitment to one's evangelistic role. A pastor must cultivate the habit of looking at the world through evangelistic glasses. One has to be on the lookout for opportunities to ask the eliciting question or to speak the witnessing word. There comes a kind of sixth sense about knowing when to affirm, confirm, or share a faith experience. A pastor is always a witness.

Theological awareness. As Samuel Calian has stated, the unique role of the pastor is to be the grass-roots theologian among the people of God.[49] If the pastor is not thinking theologically, who in the congregation is likely to be? I have always believed that one of my main functions as a minister of the Word is to teach people to think theologically. This does not come naturally for many people. We were (or should have been) trained to think theologically, but most people have not been so trained. They never went to seminary. We have to help them discern the theological issues or principles or implications implicit in a given situation, and our own theological awareness must be sharpened to do that. It is amazing how that will open up possibilities for faith sharing. A pastor is always a theologian.

A listening ear. The pastor-evangelist must be above all a good listener. Many if not most opportunities for witnessing or faith sharing are missed because we simply have not listened well. Good listening requires a genuine compassion for people; the ability to concentrate not only on what is being said but also on the face language and body language that reveal the feelings behind the words; the self-control to know when and when not to speak, and what and what not to say; the sensitivity to comprehend where the other person is coming from; the ability to clarify what is going on as well as what is being said; and a commitment to follow through in whatever ways are appropriate and helpful.[50] Who more than a pastor should have a listening ear? To be aware of faith-sharing opportunities requires that the pastor-evangelist be always a witness, always a theologian, but first and foremost always a pastor!

ACCEPTING OPPORTUNITIES

Recognizing our evangelistic opportunities is of no value if we do not avail ourselves of them. Accepting one's opportunities means taking advantage of whatever occasion presents itself and making an *appropriate* witness through whatever means we have at our disposal. A letter, a telephone call, a one-on-one conversation, a talk to a group—each of these is a medium for faith sharing. People give us many opportunities to relate to them on a heart-to-heart, faith-to-faith level. They need someone who will listen, someone who cares and who can help them to know a God who cares. To accept our evangelistic opportunities requires self-awareness, self-discipline, and self-sacrifice on the part of the pastor-evangelist.

Self-awareness. This calls for a self-inventory of our personal fears and frustrations about evangelism. What are the barriers that keep me from being a pastor-evangelist? Is it fear? A sense of inadequacy? A rejection of responsibility? A denial of the role? Whatever my personal hang-up may be, I must recognize it, confess it, and pray for God's help in overcoming it. That is the starting point. Until I do that, there is little chance of my becoming a pastor-evangelist.

Self-discipline. Next in importance is the discipline to follow through on our good intentions, to translate our noble instincts into action, to do what we know we should do and can do. We all know what road is paved with good intentions, and that is the highway I am traveling most of the time. My intentions are much better than my performance. One practice that helps a little bit is keeping a list of things I have to do, including the things I should do and the things I want to do. As I check off the things I have accomplished, the list is a visible reminder of what is yet to be done and a prod to my conscience to do them. The support of Christian friends and colleagues is extremely important also. Friends encourage us to do what we know we should. Most important of all is prayer. Without God's help I know I can never live up to my good intentions. We know we can't lift ourselves up by our own spiritual bootstraps. The goals we set for ourselves should themselves be a matter of prayer, so that our "good" intentions are God's intentions. Good habits, as everyone knows, have to be developed. One way to help cultivate the habit of evangelism is to take part in an evangelistic calling program. If there is nothing of that sort going on in one's church, one simply has to take the plunge and start paddling. You can't learn to swim if you never get into the water. Accepting evangelistic opportunities has to be understood as a matter of self-discipline.

Self-sacrifice. There is a price to pay in terms of time and energy, for a pastor-evangelist must be available to people. Not to be available is to contradict our professed interest in and concern for people. If one discovers a need one can help meet and does nothing about it, one has called the lie to one's caring. To establish a friendship and not be a friend is the rankest form of propositional evangelism. A servant of Christ is a servant of others. But serving others takes time and energy. Some pastors are not willing to make the sacrifice. A minister once said to me,

"Who needs evangelism? I've got all I can do to keep up with
my own congregation!" His congregation probably thinks the
same thing. Let's face it: Once a pastor becomes involved in
evangelism, her or his workload will increase immediately and
substantially. That reality is a barrier to many pastors. The truth
remains, however, that one cannot and should not think about
being a pastor-evangelist if one is not willing to pay the price.

MAKING OPPORTUNITIES

Being a pastor-evangelist is not a matter of sitting back and
waiting for evangelistic opportunities to come along. It will
happen that way sometimes, but more often than not we have
to make our own opportunities for witnessing. It entails having
to size up a situation and knowing where and how to plug in.
Certain human relations skills and qualities of character become
very important at this point. The basic requisites include commitment, boldness, tact, urgency, and humility.

Commitment. There has to be an intentional quality about
our evangelistic ministry. Making opportunities for faith sharing demands of us a continual, conscious commitment, both to
the task and to the Lord who calls us to the task. It requires a
conscientious desire, however imperfectly fulfilled, to be
Christ's witness at all times, in all places, in all circumstances.

Boldness. Commitment, in turn, requires boldness. A pastor-
evangelist has to be willing to take holy risks for God. Nothing
ventured, nothing gained—in evangelism as in other areas of
life. We need to be willing to broach the subject more often, to
be ready to say the word that needs to be said. How many
persons have been denied the good news by our timidity? If we
care about people, how can we not share with them the greatest
news we have to share?

Tact. Boldness without tact can be disastrous. There is a
difference between boldness and temerity. Evangelistic tact is
the ability to speak the appropriate word, at the appropriate
time, in the appropriate way, for appropriate reasons. In the
name of boldness some evangelists are anything but tactful.
They barge into people's lives like bulldozers, without a thought

or a care about the impression they make, or the response they evoke, or the feelings they hurt. They are compulsive verbalizers, convinced that their poor victim is doomed to destruction if they don't give him or her the word. The thought never crosses their mind that their words may not be *the* word, not the words that person needs to hear. If the response is not positive, it's the other person's fault, not theirs.

Urgency. Our boldness normally depends upon our sense of urgency about the task. We have to believe there is nothing more important than helping people to know, love, and serve Jesus Christ. Our time on this earth is limited and unpredictable, both for us and for the people we hope to reach. To be sure, God will work his will in people's lives when and how God chooses, with or without our help. But we can never be sure that we are not the ones God wishes to be his instruments for doing so. The precariousness of our existence demands that we be about the task for the sake of a world in desperate need of God.

Humility. But we do so with humility, knowing that God is the true Evangelist, not we. Our boldness is in the Lord, who calls us to the task. It is the boldness of faith, the boldness of one whose trust and confidence and hope are in God. Humility befits an evangelist, whose confidence is that of one who believes in and depends upon the Holy Spirit, who, as I have just said, can do his work apart from us. We are, we hope, useful to God but not indispensable. How utterly inappropriate it is for anyone to boast about evangelistic success!

We have been dealing with those personal qualities that should constrain us to be evangelists, not with techniques and skills. I am firmly convinced that once we want to be evangelists, we can be; once we are committed to faith sharing, we can surely learn to share our faith. The central theme here is that we have to be committed enough to recognize and accept the opportunities that are given to us for evangelism, and to make our own opportunities, when it is appropriate for us to take the initiative. In the next chapter we shall explore those opportunities in the context of our personal relationships.

6

The Pastor's Personal Relationships

What does it mean to be a pastor-evangelist in terms of our personal relationships? There are some very delicate and difficult issues involved, which demand of us the highest sensitivity. In terms of our faith, how should we relate to the persons closest to us? To neighbors? To friends? To parishioners? To strangers we meet? These are the questions to which we now turn.

SPOUSE AND CHILDREN

This is not a book on family counseling. We are focusing here on one main issue: the implications of being a pastor-evangelist in the context of one's own family relationships. Every situation is different, of course, and different circumstances call for different responses, different stances, and different approaches, but some general guidelines can be helpful in any situation. I have three rules, three principles, and some suggestions for *married* pastors with or without children. First the rules.

Three Rules

1. Recognize the difficulty. When there is a spiritual gap between family members, especially between spouses, it is very difficult to bridge it. This reality needs to be understood and accepted. As a pastor I have observed time and again the inability of one spouse to influence another spouse toward church, *when there is such a gap.* The gentlest, most well-intended suggestions, the subtlest hints, can evoke anger and resentment, even rage. A sweet and gentle Christian woman I know, after blowing out the candles on her birthday cake, expressed her wish that her sons would discover the joy and inspiration she had found in reading the Bible. That provoked an instant reaction from her incensed daughter-in-law, who retorted, "You're always trying to manage everyone else's life!" Shocked and hurt, the older woman wondered what she had said to arouse such a bitter outburst. When family members are on the same spiritual wavelength, or if the unchurched person is open and receptive, there may well be a positive response to such a witness. But my experience has led me to conclude that family members are often —but not always—the last persons able to handle spiritual apathy or antagonism within their own family.

2. Deal with your own guilt. The burden you carry need not be guilt. You cannot help feeling the burden of concern for a loved one who is not enjoying the relationship with God that means so much to you. It is especially painful for pastors, whose very profession only increases the burden of guilt, not to be able to share this dimension of life with those closest to them. But you and I are not solely responsible for those who must ultimately answer for themselves. We may have regrets about the things we have said or done, or failed to do or say, and to that extent have something to confess, but that is no excuse for someone else not to believe in God, no justification for rejecting Jesus Christ, the Bible, or the church.

3. Leave it to God. That is not a cop-out. It is an honest acknowledgment of our own limitations. Ultimately it is not we but God who must be the evangelist. God is the converter of human hearts. This does not release us from all responsibility in the matter, but it should relieve us of the burden of thinking it all depends on us. We ministers, like everyone else, have to learn to commit our loved ones to God's care and trust God to use our feeble attempts to be his witnesses, in his time and in his way.

Three Principles

These rules ought to be obvious to any pastor, but for some reason they are easily forgotten. Because some pastors forget the difficulty, they have a huge guilt complex about their inability to influence their spouse, or their children, or someone else for whom they feel the burden of responsibility. And in agonizing over the problem, they take the matter completely out of God's hands. Their failure to turn it over to God aggravates the guilty feelings. The following three principles may help.

1. The importance of communicating. If spouses cannot even talk about a problem, that could mean trouble down the road. Are there matters they would rather avoid than face, matters that for one or the other are too touchy or brittle? Faith talk has to be in the context of the overall relationship. If there is a good level of trust, of mutual acceptance, respect, and support, it is usually much easier to talk about matters of faith. Spouses have to grant each other the right to an opinion and respect each other's point of view. They have to acknowledge the legitimacy of each other's feelings and the sincerity of each other's convictions. The goal is mutual understanding, not agreement. Understanding each other is more important than agreeing with each other, and understanding is contingent upon communication.

2. The importance of faith. Never forget the importance of faith—your faith! Your spouse and especially your children, as they get older, can play the agnostic role as long as they know you believe. But how would they feel if you lost *your* faith? They think they can safely wander away from the church, and even from God, knowing that there is always a home port, a faith port to come home to. In a sense, you are their unacknowledged but very real spiritual security blanket, set aside for a time but always available in the closet. They know you are there, and they are content to let you do their believing for them, while they conveniently ignore their own responsibilities to God. They would probably be devastated, were you to stop believing! That is a tremendously important fact of faith, which gives us all hope and another reason for hanging in there with God.

I like to think of that as an analogy for one of the church's key roles in the world. The armchair atheists can play their little games of rejection and denial, and the barroom agnostics can indulge their pseudo-intellectual speculations, as long as there are believers in the world who point to God. If there were no believers, whom would the cynics have to attack? With whom would the agnostics argue? The unbelieving, uninvolved, unspiritual world can go on playing games as long as someone testifies to the reality of God, but what would they do if *no one* believed in God? Where would the world be then?

This realization underscores for me the importance of faith and of the integrity of our witness. The world watches to see how we Christians act and react in all the circumstances of life, and our families observe us pastors, as we experience the joys and sorrows, the ups and downs of our daily lives. It is not as important that we be able to convince them that there is a God as it is to show them by the way we think, speak, and act that *we believe there is!*

3. The importance of love. "Above all," said the apostle Peter, "hold unfailing your love for one another, for love covers a multitude of sins" (1 Peter 4:8). Indeed it does! If your spouse and your children know you love them, they will often if not usually forgive and forget your awkward efforts to encourage their faith, or at least they will put up with them as the well-intentioned efforts of an overzealous parent or spouse. Children may stray for a time, but they usually come back again, if there has been a good relationship in the home. Those bedside prayers and childhood talks about God and Jesus are important hidden ties to a way of life that was once important to them. "Faith, hope, and love abide, these three; but the greatest of these is love" (1 Cor. 13:13).

Some Suggestions

With the foregoing rules and principles in mind, here are some practical suggestions relating to the pastor's relationships with her or his family.

Be up front. Be direct but not blunt, up front, not uptight. Let your family know how you are feeling about things. Share what's in your heart.

Use "feeling" talk. It is better to share your feelings than to express your opinions. Feelings are less threatening and are less likely to put the other person on the defensive. Use "feeling" talk, not "thinking" talk.

Watch your language. Face language, that is. Avoid being or appearing to be judgmental in your attitude. Be aware of your own face language and body language and what they may be communicating. You can say the hard thing if your facial expression conveys love and acceptance. (See Chapter 11.)

Choose the context. Put your words of witness into a positive, loving context, assuming one exists. Your testimony is likely to elicit a negative response if it is done when you or others are angry.

Choose the moment. There are appropriate times for faith sharing. Choose a moment, such as an anniversary, when the mood should be one of joy and love. A time of tragedy or trouble is always an opportunity for faith sharing. It is a time for your family to see that *your* faith needs reinforcing too, a time when you need one another's strength and support. Remember, your spouse and your family almost always *want* you to believe. With children, bedtime is one of the best times for faith sharing. Most children, when they are little, would rather have their parents *put* them to bed than *send* them to bed. Bedtime can be a most meaningful time for both parents and children. It is a time to plant the seeds of faith. The seeds may have to die before they sprout and bloom in adulthood, to use Paul's imagery (1 Cor. 15:36–37), but faith has a much better chance of blooming and bearing fruit when the seeds are sown early in life.

Also, you can take advantage of what I call "neutral territories," where the right to pray has been established and is accepted by the family. These are nonthreatening occasions, such as grace at mealtimes and prayers in the car when you begin a trip or arrive safely at your destination. But don't abuse the right by preaching at them in the prayer: "Lord, help Johnny to know that it isn't nice to be messy, and teach him to clean up his room. And help Susie to stop being mean to her sister." What image of God are we helping our children to form when we do this? And don't force your spouse or one of your children to pray, one who might not want to or feel comfortable doing so. But invite and encourage them to participate in the family prayer times, so that you do not become the professional pray-er for the family, as pastors are inclined to be for groups in other settings when a prayer is needed.

Avoid religious jargon. Try not to use sanctimonious, super-pious language that reinforces the negative impressions your family may have from hearing some preachers on radio or televi-sion. With people who are turned off by the evangelical argot, I believe it is better to use God-language rather than Christ-talk. Praying in Christ's name is fine, but go easy on the evangelical lingo around people who are uncomfortable with it. And by all means avoid browbeating your family, either directly or in-directly (i.e., in prayers).

Don't nag. Don't widen the gap between you and your spouse or children by pushing too hard or harping on their spiritual failings. Nagging never works, neither do veiled references and not-so-subtle innuendos. But some people never learn that. They don't realize that the more they nag, the wider the gap becomes, so that, as I mentioned, even unintentional comments become red flags and are taken the wrong way. That's when the subject becomes taboo and communication ceases. It has become such a sore point that the persons involved avoid the subject altogether.

Don't argue in public. Never, *never,* NEVER fight your battles in public, either in open confrontation or by appealing for the consent of a third person or persons to confirm your assessment of your spouse's or child's failings. "Tell me, Bill, what do you think of a minister's wife who refuses to go to church?" Or, "My husband never wants to say grace. He always makes me do it. He's not much for religion." It is terribly embarrassing to other people and destructive of family relationships. This is especially true for pastors and their families. Be careful in the pulpit about using your children as illustrations, if it embarrasses them. And by all means don't belittle them. It is certainly necessary and desirable to pray for your family in private, expressing your desires for them to God, but always "leave it to God."

Choose your friends. Some of the churchy types who latch on to us ministers make our families want to head in the opposite direction. Choose your friends wisely, people whose faith and life-style will attract your family, not repel them, people of faith who don't wear their faith on their sleeve.

Don't criticize church members. Criticizing the church or members of the congregation in front of your children is another no-no. It can have a very negative effect on their attitude, and children cannot hide their feelings, as adults can and often do. Most pastors discover early in their ministry that the children of the congregation are the windows to the hearts of their parents. Most of the time you can tell where you stand with the parents by the way their children relate to you. Corollary: See that you don't do the same to *your* children.

Be a listener. When you talk with your spouse or children about their faith, be a *listener* first. Try to understand how they feel. Ask questions. Be interested in what they have to say. Identify with them in their struggle. Try to relate to them rather than reform them. Neither judge nor justify their negative feelings and attitudes. Understanding is what is called for.

Share your faith. The spiritual relationship between pastor and spouse begins before marriage. You should talk about your faith, your expectations of each other, how you want to relate spiritually, how you will deal with matters of faith and religious practice, how you will teach, train, and relate to your children, if you have any. These are things, incidentally, to help couples deal with in premarital counseling.

Pray! Last, but in no way least, pastors, of all people, must undergird everything they do with prayer. You and I should be praying constantly, asking for God's help in everything we do. We really do have to turn it over to God, asking him to redeem our mistakes and to use our sincere attempts to be faithful. We need to pray for patience and trust God to do his work in his own time. Maybe our spouse or daughter or son is not yet ready for God. It may not be the time *(kairos).* We should be hesitant about imposing our will on God, who knows better than we what is best for all.

PARENTS AND OTHER RELATIVES

The rules, principles, and suggestions just listed are for the most part applicable or easily adapted to your relationship with your parents, assuming you have parents. Some additional considerations should be mentioned, however.

When the Relationship Is Good

If a happy, positive relationship exists between you and your parents and the other members of your family of orientation, they are probably proud of what you are doing and of what you are, even if they may not agree with what you believe. They may unconsciously regard you as their link with the divine, their tie with the holy of holies, and maybe their ticket to heaven. They may be fond of saying, "Our daughter is a minister!" or "I have a nephew in the ministry." They can ride on your ticket, when the time comes.

When There Are Problems

Whether the relationship is good or bad, there can be problems involving conscious or unconscious feelings of resentment or guilt associated with your being what you are and doing what you do.

Family plans. There are not a few seminary students whose parents were disappointed by their decision to enter the ministry. Father may be angry that his son or daughter will not be entering the family business. The ministry has cut off one of his links to immortality, for the family business is a monument to Father's life and its continuation means the perpetuation of his name.

Life-style. A minister's life-style may be threatening to other members of the family. Your way of life may in and of itself be in their eyes a condemnation of theirs. When your priorities, values, principles, and commitments are different, that difference itself can be a source of disagreement and conflict. That is when families may end up living in a state of undeclared truce, fearfully avoiding the touchy topics that cannot be discussed without ending in a verbal battle.

Conflicting assumptions. Similarly, the premises upon which your life is now based may be totally different from those of your parents. You operate from a different set of presuppositions, and that makes communication difficult and occasionally impossible. You find yourselves talking past one another, over one another's heads, at one another, or, worst of all, *about* one another instead of *to* one another. In all interpersonal communication it is essential that each person come clean about his or her assumptions. What are the givens you have to know and accept about each other, in order to understand where the other is coming from?

Letting go. There is the problem of letting go of their children, which all parents have to some degree. When children grow up and become ministers, they form their own ideas of right and wrong, as other children do, ideas that may or may not be similar to those their parents taught them by word or by example. It is not a matter of who is right and who is wrong. It is simply the threat that their children's breaking away presents to parents—to some more than others. The problem tends to subside the longer one is out of the nest. But it is well for pastors to remember that their theological orientation and their ministerial ways may be unsettling to those who raised and supported them all through their early years, including college and maybe even seminary. This is assuming, of course, that one grew up in such a family. If not, much of what has been said is inapplicable or irrelevant.

Religious problems. There may be actual resentment over the direction you have gone or are now heading. They were Jewish; you became a Christian. They were Missouri Synod Lutherans; you became a Methodist. They believe anyone who has not been baptized by immersion is not a Christian; you practice infant baptism. They believe the denomination you belong to is apostate, or they are violently opposed to your stand on some controversial social issue.

Faith-sharing Opportunities

Those kinds of problems can make faith sharing with family members difficult, but not impossible. We ministers have to be pastors to as well as members of our families, and it is not easy to fulfill that dual responsibility. But the pastor-evangelist should be sensitive above all to the situation in his or her own home. Our theological training imposes upon us, it seems to me, the obligation to be the peacemaker in the family, the one who is always seeking to be reconciled, the one who is willing to make sacrifices and to be vulnerable for Christ's sake. So it behooves us always to be on the lookout for faith-sharing opportunities.

Mortality concerns. As parents grow older, the awareness of and sometimes preoccupation with the reality of their mortality increases and that growing awareness is often accompanied by an increased interest in religious questions, a search for ultimate meaning, and a readiness to talk. Be sensitive to that tendency. Listen for the hints and clues to those concerns, statements such as "Well, I'm not going to live to see it" or "I'm not going to be around much longer" or "This may be my last Christmas." An appropriate response might be "Does that worry you?" or "How do you feel about that?" or "What if it should be your last Christmas?" Such a question can lead to a beautiful faith-sharing conversation, which might be further prompted by another question at the right moment (i.e., if it feels comfortable and natural and seems appropriate), such as "As you think back over your life, what do you want to be remembered for?" or "How do you want people to remember you?" or "What things have mattered most to you in life?" Older folks like to philosophize and to feel that their ideas and experiences are appreciated and worth listening to. Affirm them in the telling and, as appropriate, plug in with your own faith experience, what is important to you. If they show an increased interest in spiritual things or give evidence of a new awareness of God, let them know that nothing could make you happier.

Crisis calls. Parents and relatives who otherwise have shown no great interest in your ministry will often call you when there is a crisis or a need of some kind—a death, a serious illness, an accident, or a major decision (such as whether to sell their house and go into a retirement home, where to live after retirement, what to do about Grampa). You may be asked to officiate at a wedding, perform a baptism, conduct a funeral, or make a pastoral call, all of which requests are opportunities for sharing faith with the person who asks you, as you seek to be helpful. Planning a funeral service, for example, though there may be great sorrow, can be a most meaningful time for family sharing.

Acceptable occasions. These are those neutral territories I mentioned, those times when your "right" to pray is expected and affirmed, such as at mealtimes, on a hospital call, or at religious services. But be sensitive about what and how you pray —and about how long. The same principles also apply with respect to "preaching" in prayers; avoid it like the plague!

Live-in Parents or Relatives

When parents or relatives are living in your home, the problems are often compounded. Tensions can build up among different generations of people living under the same roof. There are similar considerations as with one's spouse and children, with the additional factors I have mentioned regarding the special needs of older people. There are also these considerations:

Head-of-household conflicts. It is difficult sometimes for parents to relinquish their role as head of the household and take a subordinate role in their son's or daughter's home. The need to feel important is still there, and they want to feel they are contributing to the family and not a burden to it. Sometimes they demand attention, and, like children, they sometimes try to get it by being cantankerous.

Congregational pressures. Live-in relatives may feel the same pressure that your spouse and children feel is imposed upon them because of their relation to you as pastor, especially if you and they are living in a parsonage, rectory, or manse and not in your own home. They need to be protected from the kinds of pressures and demands that parishioners do indeed sometimes impose upon ministers' families by their critical comments and odious comparisons.

The positive side. It is to be hoped that those living with you will see and share the joy of your faith. Here is where the witness of your life is so important. They will have a firsthand opportunity to observe you in all kinds of situations, and they may discover, if they don't already know it, that a faith relationship with God and Jesus Christ is an uplifting, happy experience. They will see that, if your own faith walk is genuine.

Correspondence with Relatives

Some people can say things better in writing than they can in person. They figure they have more time to think about, correct, and improve a written communiqué. Letters are an important medium for faith sharing. Pastor-evangelists are as sensitive about what they write as about what they say. That should apply to family correspondence as much as to any other. Give careful thought both to the content and to the timing of your letters. Remember birthdays and anniversaries, which provide opportunities for a low-key witness. This is usually more effective than a hard-sell approach. It is a good idea to send printed copies of your sermons (you will know best whether they are worth sending), which are usually read by the recipient. Church bulletins and newsletters are also good mailing pieces. Sending such items is effective because:

• Those to whom you send them do not feel the sermon was "aimed" at them. They are not threatened, because they know you preached it to your congregation.

• It is likely to be read because *you* wrote it. What's more, they often share it with others.

• Your unchurched parents or relatives, therefore, will be reading the good news, provided you have been preaching it!

• They tend to keep your sermons and often refer to them again, when a particular need or problem arises that you have addressed.

With regard to relationships with his or her family and relatives, then, the pastor-evangelist should be as sensitive and tactful, yet as forthright, in bearing witness to them as he or she is to anyone else—even more so, because of the factors I have mentioned. We should use the same discretion, wisdom, and tact with our family as we would with others, in deciding when, where, and how to broach the subject of faith.

FRIENDS

Again, the same general rules and principles apply. Some people think, however, that it is more difficult to witness to friends because of the risks involved. Here are some things to keep in mind.

Be Direct

Whatever you may be feeling about talking with a friend, let that feeling be the starting point of your witness.

"Harry, we've known each other all these years, and I've never had the courage to ask you about what I feel is the most important thing in one's life, because I didn't want to offend you."

"What's that?"

"Your faith. What do you believe about God? About the church? About Christ?"

Or, "Betty, you are a very important person to me, a special friend whom I dearly love and respect, and I know you realize that. But there is one dimension of life we've never shared or talked about, and for me it's the most important part of my life. I'm talking about my faith in God. How do you feel about God? Do you believe?"

You can express it in words that feel comfortable to you. The point is to be up front about it. Let the other person know what you are feeling. Your friends, like your relatives, may not agree with you, but they respect you for believing. They are impressed by what your faith means to you. And they, like your relatives, may turn to you in time of need. That has happened to me many times, with friends from preministry days as well as current acquaintances. Use such opportunities wisely, tactfully, and well.

Be Low Key

With friends, as with relatives, we should not let our faith get in the way. If they feel judged by us, uncomfortable at best and resentful at worst, our attempts to witness can erode the relationship and become a barrier instead of a bridge to communication. You don't want to be a wet blanket. One way to share your faith is to let them know that you are praying for them, but do it in a way that is neither condescending nor superficial. Correspondence and telephone calls are just as important mediums of communication with friends as they are with family maybe more so, as it is not likely that we can keep up with all our friends by personal visits. Give thought to what you say in your greeting cards and letters. Low-key it!

Reunions

Class and other types of reunions often present opportunities for faith sharing with friends, especially as the years roll on and old friends are fewer. Your college friends will often seek you out in the midst of reunion revelry and engage you in a heart-to-heart conversation about their lives, their troubles, their disappointments and accomplishments, their faith. At my last major college reunion I had several conversations with classmates who wanted to tell me about their battles with alcohol. Out of their common concern about some of our classmates, whose behavior betrayed a real need in this area, grew a network of support for any member of our class needing and wanting help. Another important feature of our five-year reunions is our class memorial service, held in the college chapel. It is a beautiful experience for all who come—solemn and impressive, and yet with a note of joy. What an opportunity for me to present the gospel to my classmates and their spouses, some of whom never darken the door of a church! In the context of that memorial service I have an opportunity to raise and address the deepest questions of life and faith, of meaning and purpose, of past, present, and future, with classmates who sit surrounded by the sobering reality of the transitory nature of our existence on this earth. Out of those

services have come the opportunities for one-on-one conversations with many who are searching for meaning and for answers
to ultimate questions.

The crew of the ship on which I served in World War II has
an annual reunion, which I have never attended but which has
been the occasion for some interesting conversations and correspondence with those who plan the event. I have watched the
growing spiritual emphasis over the years, and I am sure that
if I attended, there would be all kinds of opportunities for faith
sharing.

PARISHIONERS

The same rules and principles apply, but again there are
unique aspects of a pastor-parishioner relationship that need to
be kept in mind.

Desire for Friendship

Most people want to be friends with their pastor. They *will*
be, if you give them half a chance. They will take you into their
confidence. They want you to understand them, approve of
them, like them. It is one of the tremendous advantages of being
a pastor.

The Trust Factor

People want to and *do* trust their pastor. How tragic it is
when a pastor betrays that trust. Your people want to believe
in you, in your sincerity, your integrity, your honesty. These
qualities are much more important to them than your intellectual prowess.

Community Acceptance

It is still true in America that your pastoral calling grants you
instant access to many people's homes and hearts. You don't
have the problem most lay people have when they move into a

new community. You are invited to join this group and that. Your profession is an entrée. Be aware of your built-in acceptance, but do not abuse or misuse it. Many of the people you come to know through these contacts will visit your church, and some, maybe many, will become your parishioners. A relationship has been established, but what are the subtle differences in that relationship *after* you become their pastor? The changes are not easily predictable, but they are often easily discernible!

Parishioner Expectations

Your pastoral role carries with it certain professional responsibilities that are assumed and accepted by your parishioners, who *expect* you to be there when they need you. That expectation is more an asset than a liability, a privilege as well as a responsibility. Whereas with other people you may have to win your right of access, you can assume that right with your parishioners. They understand that your pastoral position imposes upon you the duty as well as the right to be there, and that is a tremendous advantage. In crisis situations your friends may or may not turn to you for spiritual support, but your parishioners automatically do so, unless they have rejected you as their pastor. But even then, they will, reluctantly perhaps, allow you to be there and do what a pastor does. A time of crisis is often the very best time for reconciliation, for the fact that you are there, wanting to be helpful, shows that you are not letting any negative feelings they suspect you have toward them (their own guilt convinces them you must have such feelings!) prevent you from being a pastor to them in their time of need.

Other Considerations

Doubt and the faithful. The faithful have their doubts! Most church people have far more questions and doubts about their faith than some of us pastors seem to realize. We operate from our own set of assumptions and often miss the real questions, which people wish we would answer but which they are too afraid, embarrassed, or timid to ask. There is some agnosticism in most of us, and much agnosticism in some of us who call ourselves Christians. As preachers we must remember this, lest we continually talk over the heads and hearts of our people. As counselors we need to be alert to signs of doubt and disbelief, so that our words don't have a hollow ring to those who do not share our assumptions or understand our pious language.

Faith sharing in the parish. Parishioners need to be encouraged and taught to share their faith with one another. In your preaching and teaching ministry it is important to wrestle early and often with the meaning, nature, and role of faith, emphasizing and illustrating the validity of one's personal experience of God and stressing the givenness of faith. The pastor should facilitate faith sharing in church board meetings and whenever and wherever parishioners gather for study, prayer, fellowship, or church business. In your counseling or calling, and in all phases of pastoral care, be sensitive to opportunities for faith sharing. Ask questions that free others to relate their faith to their life's experiences and to talk about their faith struggles, their understanding of Christian discipleship, their doubts and fears, their joys and sorrows, and how all these are affecting the way they perceive God and relate to God. Your role as pastor allows you to do this and gives you opportunities to do so, more with your parishioners than with anyone else.

The turf factor. Oftentimes the best place for this kind of conversation to happen is on *their* turf rather than on yours. Their defenses may be up when they come to your study at the church. They see you in a role that conditions and may predetermine their reactions and responses. But if you show up at their places of employment, or in their homes, they tend to be more secure in their own surroundings and consequently perceive you differently. First of all, they are *usually* (not always) pleased and flattered that you would come to them. Second, they sense the importance you attach to them and to whatever it is that brings you there, such as to ask them to take on a particular task in the church, to deal with a misunderstanding, or to inquire about some problem or need they may have. Third, they are usually (not always) more honest and up front on their own turf. The security of familiar surroundings frees them to be that way.

In the fourth place, I find that they are more willing to share their faith on their own turf. Your coming to their office, for example, symbolizes in a tangible way the relation between their faith and their occupation. As one layman laughingly put it, "The holy one has invaded my secular world!" Most lay people have many questions about how their faith relates to their work and how what they believe affects what they do, but these questions may never have surfaced, may never have been sorted out and dealt with, until you arrived on the scene.

Once when I needed some work done on my car, I took it to a repair shop where the service manager happened to be an inactive member of my congregation. We had had very little contact up to that point. When I went to pick up the car, he invited me into his office, presumably to discuss the bill, but instead he wanted to talk about God. This was the same man about whom another church member commented, "Larry's a nice man, but you'll never see him in church!" Larry had many questions and much that he wanted to get off his chest. In that instance I had not initiated the conversation, but he did, and what a conversation it was! The following Sunday he was in church, and every Sunday from then on.

The unfriendly parishioner. There is much more truth than fiction in the old saying, "You can't win 'em all!" If you are preaching the gospel faithfully, you are bound to offend or upset somebody sometime.

> Just preach what they like and how lovely it goes;
> The honeymoon lasts till you step on their toes!

The level of the reaction depends on the sensitivity of the corn. Sometimes you will hear the "Ouch!" Other times you won't hear it, and you won't know it. Accept the fact that you can't do everything or be everywhere. You are bound to miss seeing someone in the hospital, or forget to call someone you should have called, or find yourself someplace when somebody thinks you should have been somewhere else. You cannot always say the right thing (as others define it), act the right way, have the right attitude or opinion about everything, wear the right clothes, socialize with the right people, spend your leisure time in the right manner, or have a spouse and children who look, act, and behave exactly right at all times, in all places, and under all circumstances. So accept the fact that no matter how popular you may be with some or even most people, you can't win 'em all!

So what do you do about the ones you don't win? You go on loving them. You may not like them, you may disagree with what they say or do, but you don't stop loving them. They are God's children too, and you are their pastor. So be there when they need you, and go on ministering as best you can. If the criticism is false, the best way to counteract it is to show by your actions that it isn't true. You may not stop the criticism, but you can certainly cut down on its effects.

Pastors, of all people, should be fair in their dealings with their enemies and critics. Being fair includes not impugning others' motives or questioning their integrity. It is hard not to do that sometimes. You and I may not be objective, but we can and should be fair, as we interpret their position to our would-be friends and supporters.

An important lesson every pastor has to learn is how to absorb criticism. There is no sport in punching a pillow. As long as you fight back, your critics will keep pounding away at you. The best defense may be a good offense in basketball but not in pastoral relations. For a pastor, the best defense many times is no defense. It is better not to play the critics' game. Rather, as Paul advised Timothy, set the believers an example in speech and conduct (1 Tim. 4:12).

It is a good policy to deal with people on a face-to-face basis, if they will let you. Talk *to* them, not about them. Say to their face what you want to say, not behind their back, even though they may be doing that to you. And if you possibly can, deal with the problem, whatever it is, on a faith-sharing basis. Look at it together with whoever is opposing you in the light of your joint responsibility to be reconciled, to be Christ's faithful disciples, and to obey his commandment to love one another as he has loved us.

A final suggestion regarding unfriendly parishioners: Ask for their help. Let them know they are needed. Ask a favor or give them a task to do, some responsibility whereby they can make a contribution to the life of the church. In so doing you provide an opportunity for them to save their pride, or to salve their conscience, or to climb down from whatever limb they've been out on. Ask a favor of an enemy, and you will often make a friend!

STAFF

What if you are part of a multiple staff in a large church where there is a colleague who is opposed to evangelism? What if he or she has a faith problem? There are not a few ministers who are uncomfortable with God language, who cannot talk about or share their personal experience of God and resent those who do. What if a colleague is in trouble or has a desperate need of some kind? What if she or he has a debilitating guilt complex and whatever has caused it is too personal and intimate to discuss?

My conversations with ministers in multiple-staff churches have convinced me that such questions are more the rule than the exception. There is no intention here to delve deeply into the complexities of staff relationships. Recognizing that much of what has been said in the preceding sections is applicable here as well, I simply want to list a few general guidelines with specific reference to the pastor-evangelist's relationships with staff colleagues.

1. Keep it private. Woe to staff members who fight their private battles in public! Colleagues should respect one another's confidences and never violate one another's trust. There is nothing more devastating to the morale of a congregation than distrust, hostility, and enmity within the pastoral staff. It is sad but true that the biggest problem in most large churches is staff relationships. Ministers should be the first persons to understand the importance of working out their problems among themselves, but too many staff members are building their own little kingdoms. The result is an unhealthy jealousy and rivalry, which in turn give rise to the political maneuvering and manipulating that is so destructive to congregational health.

2. Pray together. To paraphrase the cliché, the staff that prays together stays together. Prayer is the context in which dreams should be shaped and shared, failures confessed and forgiven, needs recognized and addressed, help given and received, appreciation expressed, and successes celebrated. Praying staff members remember whose church it is and affirm their obedience to the one Lord, who called each of them into his service and whose ministry they share.

3. Share faith. The pastor-evangelist should try to encourage faith sharing among the staff, looking for plug-in points, just as he or she would with anyone else. Affirming the other person's ministry will often evoke a faith response, when that person in turn gives the credit to God, as modesty would prescribe. Why not take time in staff meetings to share experiences of answered prayer or the miracles of God's grace that one has observed in one's ministry that week?

4. Be available. If you have been praying and sharing together, your colleagues will know that you care and that you are available to them, and they will turn to you in time of need. What a privilege and joy it is to have such a relationship with one's colleagues! And how much more effective in ministry each will be as a result!

5. Be honest. In staff relationships, as in all others, honesty is the best policy. It is important to recognize and to discuss theological differences, in order that they may be dealt with positively and realistically. Differences of opinion are to be expected, and conflict can be healthy. But there are some matters upon which agreement is essential to harmonious relationships and to the peace and unity of the church. Glaring differences in their pastors' life-styles can be confusing and disconcerting to a congregation. A sharp contrast in their Christological affirmations can be a source of division in a church, where there are always people seeking to divide and conquer.

STRANGERS

We should be sensitive to opportunities for faith sharing in the various secular settings in which we find ourselves. If we live and act as concerned Christians, sensitive to human need and interested in others and available to them, strangers will often seek us when they are troubled or perplexed. Ministers have the same opportunities as lay people to be witnesses, as well as some others our very profession makes possible for us. People with problems, upon discovering you are a minister, will often engage you in conversation. The topic may be a smoke screen as they feel you out, but a sensitive pastor can often cut through the screen and free the person to say what's on his or her heart.

You may be reading a theology book on an airplane, and your seatmate will initiate a conversation, having noticed what you are reading. "Are you a minister? I see you're reading a religious book" (as if other people don't read religious books). The point is that the person may have something she or he would like to say, and it's easier to talk about some things when you are thirty thousand feet in the air than when you are on the ground.

Some Thoughts About Witnessing to Strangers

Don't waste time. Cocktail conversation is a pleasant pastime for those who enjoy it but an ineffective medium for evangelism. Religious bull sessions bore me, and I don't have time to waste arguing about religion. I learned early in my ministry that religious arguments are singularly unproductive. You cannot argue someone into the kingdom. You may win the argument and lose the person, especially if that person is a stranger. There are far more constructive ways to spend your time than arguing with people who are not really interested in wrestling with the truth and probing their faith. Be available, of course, to those who need and want your help with a problem; but you don't need to spend your precious time with people who just like to hear themselves talk. Before you terminate the conversation, however, give them a chance to respond by saying, "Look, I'd like to visit with you, if you really want to talk about your faith, but I'm not interested in arguing about religion."

Follow through. That is not always easy or even possible to do with strangers. But if there is any possible way to follow through on your chance evangelistic contacts—with a telephone

call, or a note, or a referral—it is very important to do so. It's
the follow-up that can make the difference in the stranger's mind
between an interesting conversation soon to be forgotten and a
sincere witness by someone who really did mean it. Involve
others as available and appropriate in the follow-through process.

End on a positive note. If there is no chance to follow through
on the contact, then simply terminate the conversation positively and appropriately with a sensitive exhortation, invitation,
suggestion, personal statement, or whatever seems best at the
time. "Since we'll probably never see each other again, I just
want to say that I hope you'll look for a church when you move
to your new community, and I'll be praying that God will help
you with (whatever the person's need or problem)."

Pray for the person. The stranger with whom you shared
faith should be on your prayer list, at least for a time. Invite
some intercessory prayer group to pray for that person also,
along with other strangers whose names you give them from
time to time. It is essential to water the seeds you have planted.
Who knows what fruits may come from such faith-sharing encounters with strangers?

Pray for yourself. Pray that God will use your efforts to be
his witness, that he will redeem your mistakes and forgive your
hesitancy and timidity, or your overeagerness, aggressiveness,
and insensitivity. Pray that you will learn from each experience
and do better the next time. Pray for God to give you new
opportunities for witnessing and enable you to respond in the
most appropriate way to each situation. In a word, pray!

Walk-ins

Strangers often show up at the church, seeking counseling or
inquiring about a baptism or a wedding. These are your best
opportunities with strangers, and they can and should often lead
to church membership. An unchurched couple looking for a
minister to marry them ought to be prime prospects. As you
contract with them regarding premarital counseling, you have
a wonderful opportunity to teach them and to lead them into a

relationship with Christ, as they discuss the meaning of their marital vows and look at their marriage from a Christian perspective. If most of the couples you decide to marry do not become church members by the time of the wedding, then you really have not been much of a pastor-evangelist.

So, too, with those who inquire about having their child baptized. If they are willing to participate in your prebaptism instruction class, there is every reason to hope that they will come to a decision about their own faith and their relation to the church. If they do not, then they themselves can usually see the incongruity of having their child baptized. In infant baptism it is, of course, the parents who take the vows. The purpose of the instruction is to give integrity to their words, as they think seriously and deeply about what it means to confess Jesus Christ as their personal Lord and Savior and about their responsibility to bring up their child to know, love, and obey Christ.

Transients

A special word needs to be said about transients, those who wander into the church looking for a handout. Depending on the location of your church, you can have many or few of them. There are some realities to be recognized.

They almost never tell the truth. That may sound cynical, but it is an observation born of many, many experiences with transients. My best advice is to listen sympathetically but don't be taken in by their story. They tell you what they think will evoke from you the response they want (usually money). There may be elements of truth in the tale—yes, they are passing through town and down on their luck—but they seldom give you the real reasons and never the whole truth. They are the most manipulative human beings on earth, great storytellers, and experts at making you feel sorry for them.

They do have a need. Usually but not always the need is financial. They are often down and out, even desperate. Certainly the church should be prepared to help such people, and members of the congregation should be enlisted to participate in the ministry to transients. Depending on the number and the need, the church may want to run its own soup kitchen for down-and-outers, along with a used clothing center and whatever other services are called for. That some human beings are reduced to asking for handouts is itself enough indication that they have a need. But there are also con artists who make a good living by begging from churches. They know the soft touches, and they go from church to church. When you suspect that is the case, it is a good idea to check with the neighboring churches to see if they have already been hit or to warn them that they might be. Begging from churches is a popular racket. Even so, those who do it for dishonest reasons have a need as much as those who do it out of desperation. It is unlikely that you will be able to help the con artists with their real need, for they don't want that kind of help.

Relating to transients. The same general rules of interpersonal witnessing apply to transients that apply to everyone else, starting with the importance of listening. The pastor-evangelist must first be a listener. The second rule is to be up front with them. "Look, I don't need to know your life story. I believe you need help, and perhaps we can help you, if you really want us to. If you are planning to settle down in our town, we may be able to help you find work and a place to live. If you are just passing through, we can get you a meal, a place to spend the night, and some gas for your car." It's interesting how many of these transients have cars!

They don't want a sermon. Your best witness is to represent a church that cares and is willing to help if they will accept it. That means establishing a relationship in which you can do for them what you can do only if they keep in contact and are willing to cooperate. The trouble is that most of them do not want that kind of help.

What they want is money, but that's the last thing you should give them. Instead, have arrangements with a nearby restaurant where they can get a meal (set a limit!), with a gas station where they can get a tank of gas or so many dollars' worth, and with a place or places where they can spend the night (such as the Salvation Army, a rescue mission, or a room at the church).

If they do seem to have a need for spiritual support, and if they are open and receptive, by all means bear witness to the transforming power and love of God. Your approach depends on the need, as you perceive it. That requires sensitivity on your part, as well as perceptiveness. Look for come-in points and plug-in points (see Chapter 11), but don't be fooled by their response. Most transients are experts at making an unsuspecting pastor feel they are really listening and interested in what he or she has to say. For a few dollars they will even put up with a bit of sermonizing. It goes with the territory.

Not often but occasionally you will encounter someone whom you really can help, someone who is honest about his or her situation and is not giving you a long song and dance. When such a person happens by and you are able to be of help, Hallelujah! One such experience makes up for many disappointments.

The focus here has been upon those individuals who are indeed transients. If they are located in the community, where there is a possibility for follow-up, then the church has a Christian obligation to do whatever it can to be of help to the individuals who come seeking it.

We have been exploring what it means to be a pastor-evangelist in terms of our personal relationships, moving from our most intimate associations to our chance meetings with strangers. In the next chapter we shall consider some of the more important situational factors that describe the context of evangelism and therefore should inform a pastor's evangelistic style.

7
The Pastor's Contextual Considerations: Age

One obvious factor to be considered in doing the work of an evangelist is the age of the person or persons to whom we are relating. Are there differences in the way we should relate, for example, to an audience of junior high young people and to an audience of senior citizens? Are there special considerations in witnessing to children as against young adults or middle-aged persons? The answer to these questions is clearly yes. Identifying those differences is a much more difficult matter, but one does not have to be an expert in the fields of child psychology, adolescent behavior, and geriatrics, or know everything there is to know about parenting, or the youth culture, or any other related area of the behavioral sciences, in order to do evangelism. To be sure, one can learn from these disciplines, and the more informed one is about them the better. The purpose of this chapter, however, is to suggest some general guidelines for the pastor who would like to witness more effectively to persons of different ages. Our focus is evangelism, not psychology.

CHILDREN

Let us begin with the art of relating to children—and I am convinced it is more of an art than a skill. I am referring to the preadolescent years, infancy to sixth grade. To relate to children —or, to put it more accurately, in order for them to relate to you—the following rules are basic:

They must sense that you love them and enjoy them. This means that you must genuinely love and enjoy them! If you don't, forget about relating. Children have an uncanny sixth sense about insincerity. They are not fooled by phony facades and pretentious affection.

They must sense that you are comfortable with them. Again, you must indeed be comfortable with them. Not all adults are. Being comfortable includes the ability to be silly without forfeiting your authority or compromising your credibility. Children will let you make the transition from silliness to seriousness, if you know when and how to be one or the other. For an example I think immediately of comedian Bill Cosby, whose television commercials reveal his natural gift for relating to children. Some ministers can give children's sermons and some cannot. Those who cannot should not! If you don't feel comfortable in that role, let someone else give the children's sermon, if you must have a children's sermon. Whoever does it should be able to relate to children on their level. It helps to be funny, but the humor should be aimed at them, not at the adults in the congregation.

They must see you as a likable person. This means that you must be a person children can like. What kind of person is that?

One who does not come on too strong, too fast, or too soon. Give them a chance to size you up, especially in one-on-one situations. Let the child make the first move. But you can pave the way for that with a smile, a wink, a trick, a silly expression, or some other gesture by which you do not impose but offer yourself. Children back off if you try to force yourself upon them. Instead, try to catch their interest, and they'll usually come around.

One who stimulates the child's imagination. A child knows how to pretend and can move into and out of the world of fantasy with ease. Let your own sense of wonder appeal to theirs by the tone of your voice, your facial expression, your gestures. It is so easy to relate to children if you haven't forgotten what it's like to be a child! Maybe that is part of what Jesus meant when he said, "Unless you turn and become like children, you will never enter the kingdom of heaven" (Matt. 18:3).

One who can tell a story well. Children love stories, but telling them is a risky enterprise. There are some definite dos and don'ts. Be careful, for example, how you ask questions in a

children's sermon. You can get some embarrassing answers
sometimes. One preacher called the children to the front of the
sanctuary, seated them on the chancel steps, and began his story
of David and Goliath by announcing that he was going to tell
them about a famous fight. "Have you ever seen a fight?" he
asked, innocently enough. Whereupon little Allison volun-
teered, "My mommy and daddy had a fight last night. Mommy
threw a lamp at Daddy, and then Daddy—" It was difficult to
tell who was the most embarrassed, the pastor, the congregation, or the little girls' parents, who were sitting in the first pew.
Allison was quickly interrupted, and there were no more questions that morning.

Another "don't" in telling stories to children is moralizing.
Let the story be its own message. Unlike most adults, little
children cannot think analogically or understand abstract principles drawn from stories. I believe most preachers can learn to
tell Bible stories well. Stories are the doorway to a child's heart,
especially stories about Jesus. Adults like stories too, as the
interest in narrative theology attests. The promoters of that
theological fad have been going to elaborate lengths to tell us
what most effective preachers have known for a long, long time
—that people respond to the telling of stories, especially when
they can see how *the* story relates to their story.

One whose ministerial role does not get in the way. Let the
children see you in your clerical garb, if you wear such, in other
settings than the pulpit, so that their only impression of you in
a robe is not one of authority, mystery, mystification, and even
intimidation. I think it is a good idea to mingle with them in the
fellowship hall sometimes, before removing your robe after the
worship service. Let them see you laughing at, listening to, and
caring for people. Visit their classrooms in your robe now and
then. Do your silly routine in your clerical garb, so that their
reaction to you in your vestments is not one of fear and shyness.
On the contrary, your clerical garb should be, for the children
of your congregation, a symbol that connotes and evokes friendliness, warmth, understanding, and love. That kind of exposure
does wonders for your relationship with the little folks in your
church, who will see you as the same person in the pulpit that

they have come to know and love in other settings.
They must sense what you are about. This means that you
must *know* what you are about! As a pastor-evangelist you
should want the children, as well as the adults, to know what
is important to you, and what is important to you is being a
disciple of Jesus Christ. Your desire is to help children in their
way and at their level to know what it means to belong to the
family of faith, to know Jesus as a friend, and to experience that
relationship as a joyful, happy privilege and a challenging responsibility. You want them to begin to understand what it
means to be a disciple of Christ, so that one day they can commit
their lives to him as their personal Lord and Savior. That's what
you should be about as a pastor-evangelist to children, and
everything you do should foster that intention. You will, of
course, adjust your language and style to the level of the children involved. Relating to three-year-olds is not the same as
relating to twelve-year-olds. But the same general principles
pertain, and the ultimate goal is the same.

YOUTH

Many seminary students are doing fieldwork as youth advis-
ers in local churches. I once asked an assembled group of them
for their observations about evangelizing junior and senior high
school students. Their responses were perceptive and remarkably consistent. Youth evangelism, they agreed, must be relational and incarnational. "They need to know you care, and that
you are aware of and understand their struggles. You have to
share with them that you've had the same kinds of struggles, and
then show them how your faith has helped you. You have to be
with them and enter into their lives. And the fewer rules the
better!"

"What qualities does that call for in us?" I asked. The responses: "Openness. . . . The ability to love those who don't love
you. . . . The willingness to risk, to accept criticism, to share
your beliefs. . . . Above all, you have to be a person of prayer.
God gives you insights and enables you to do things you could
never do on your own."

To these wise utterances I want to add some thoughts of my own, born of my own experience in relating to youth over the years as a teacher and coach, as a student assistant minister to junior highs, as one actively involved in the Fellowship of Christian Athletes for many years, as a pastor, as a parent, and as one who has not completely forgotten what it was like to be a teenager. Admittedly, the zest of youth has faded with time, but the memories linger on!

Plug-in Points

First let me suggest some of the principal plug-in points in relating to young people.

Their idealism. It is not wise to generalize about the attitudes of young people, because their prevailing or dominant moods vary from generation to generation. Indeed, they are constantly changing. What a contrast between the patriotism that characterized the youth of the early 1940s and the militant anti-institutionalism displayed by the youth of the late 1960s. How different is the youth view of the future in this nuclear age from that of young people before the atom bomb. We have seen the transition from hyperactivism to the narcissism of the "me-first" generation, from a deeply concerned social consciousness to a self-indulgent hedonism, reflected in the music of the drug culture, as punk rock and heavy metal displace the protest songs of the 1960s and early 1970s. One must ask, furthermore, which young people those who generalize have in mind. Are they white, black, Hispanic, or Asian? Are they preppies or street kids? Are they from the Bronx or Malibu Beach?

I believe, nevertheless, that there is in almost all young people an innate idealism. I am using this not as a philosophical but as an ethical term. I am thinking of their sense of justice, fairness, their desire for what is right. It may be and often is stifled by their environment, but there is an incipient idealism in young people that too many adults ignore or overlook. I am sure there are important cultural and environmental considerations, but I have been told by those who have lived and labored among the most deprived peoples on earth that even in the midst of starvation they have seen this quality. It is certainly true of most American youth, who still have their hopes and dreams. The opposite of ethical idealism is not realism but cynicism. There is much of that too, and we must understand it.

But we don't plug into it. Rather, we should appeal to a young person's better self. That's how Jesus related to people. He appealed to their best selves. He understood their weaknesses, but he challenged their strengths. When I have remembered to do that with young people, I have seldom been disappointed by their response. Their idealism is a vital plug-in point.

Their need for a cause. Young people need something to believe in, to belong to, something to which they can give themselves wholeheartedly, about which they can get excited. What better cause have we to offer them than the cause of Jesus Christ? The world needs a Savior! There is nothing more important to which they can give themselves than helping people to know, to love, and to obey Jesus Christ.

Their need for heroes. *Sports Illustrated* magazine referred to the Fellowship of Christian Athletes as "hero worship harnessed." Young people need heroes, big brothers and sisters who serve as role models. Pastors are in a position to be role models for many young people. To ignore that reality is a tragic mistake. Jesus said, "Whoever causes one of these little ones who believe in me to sin, it would be better for [that person] to have a great millstone fastened round [the] neck and to be drowned in the depth of the sea" (Matt. 18:6). I can remember my boyhood heroes and their influence on my life. The pastor as evangelist should plug into youth's need for someone to idolize by introducing them to the one "hero" worth their total loyalty, highest devotion, and complete trust, the one hero who will never let them down—Jesus Christ!

Their need for peer acceptance. Most adults are well aware of the tremendous impact of peer pressure. Young people want to be liked and accepted by their peers. In his book *Junior High Ministry,* Wayne Rice reported that in a nationwide survey of more than seven hundred junior high young people, by far the most important question for them was "Do you like me?"[51] There is no doubt that one of the most determinative influences

on the behavioral patterns of the majority of young people is
peer pressure. That being the case, the best way to reach young
people is through the young people who influence them: their
leaders. Young Life, Youth for Christ, Campus Crusade, and
other Christian youth ministries make much use of this principle. They know that young people do not like to be different.
The typical teenager would rather be one of the crowd than
stand out. To be cool is not to be exceptional but to be accepted.
When the church is perceived by young people as the place to
go and the thing to do, young people will come. Who goes there
determines who comes there.

The truth of that statement was dramatically underscored by
my own experience as a pastor in connection with a Young Life
youth study project in which our church was involved with four
other churches of various denominations. The purpose of the
three-year project was to discover how some of the effective
methods and principles of Young Life's ministry to youth could
be adapted to the local church. When the immensely popular
Young Life area director joined our ministerial staff as youth
director, we were sure that the more than fifty young people in
our congregation who were relating to Young Life rather than
to our own senior high fellowship would automatically become
involved in the latter, such was their affection for the director.
The astounding fact was that not one of those young people
came! Even the magnetism of the youth director could not
overcome the peer pressure. The Young Life kids simply did not
identify with the youth fellowship kids. The leaders were in
Young Life and that's where they went. Who goes decides who
comes! Young people tend to do what other young people do.

Their need for understanding. Young people have their own
struggles, pressures, and problems, as we have said. Here are
some plug-in points for the sensitive pastor.

The search for identity. This is a basic human need that is
particularly strong in young people. They wonder, Who am I?
Why am I here? Where did I come from, and where am I going?
They are wrestling with their sexuality and the pressures this
imposes. They must make the difficult transition from childhood
through the agonies of adolescence to adulthood. They struggle

with the perplexities of educational and vocational decision-making, often with choices limited by economic deprivation or their personal or environmental circumstances. What do I want to do with my life? What can I do? How grateful they are for a sensitive adult who will listen and try to understand! What a precious opportunity for us pastors, who know about a Christ in whom one can discover one's true humanity and find one's proper identity.

Family struggles. Young people's search for identity is complicated by their family struggles—sibling rivalries, parental pressures, and family feuds. They are caught in the tension between their desire to break away and the reality of their dependence. In the mystifying dynamics of the love-hate relationship, they must share the impact of financial worries, health problems, death, and dying. They need someone outside the family circle to whom they can talk, and who can help them understand the painful realities of life.

Faith questions. Many young people wonder what they can believe in, what is "for sure." They are caught in the desperate tension between their need to ask questions and their desire to know, between their skepticism and their gullibility, between their need to be regimented and their desire to experiment, between the pressure to conform and the longing to be free, between their craving for affection and their fear of rejection, between their eagerness and their reluctance to grow up, between their professions and their performance, between their self-esteem and their self-hatred. How desperately they need someone who understands this tension, someone who they sense really knows and really cares. The pastor as evangelist should, by listening and caring, convey to them the good news that there *is* a Friend who understands, who accepts them as they are and loves them as they are—Jesus Christ!

Their need to laugh. Young people appreciate and respond to humor. It is a most useful and effective plug-in point. But the humor must be at their level. They will laugh at things that relate to their own experience. This is not intended to be an analysis of the phenomenon of humor. It is simply to emphasize what anyone who has ever worked with young people knows:

that humor is an invaluable asset in relating to people of any age, but especially to young people. We need to show them that fellowship with Jesus Christ is a joyful experience, and that Christians can laugh at themselves and at life. We need to disabuse them of the notion that Christianity is for deadbeats, dumbbells, dingbats, and dingalings. The God of creation must have had a sense of humor or he wouldn't have made giraffes!

Their music. If you want to relate to young people, you had better relate to their music, especially in any kind of mass evangelism where music is part of the program. You don't have to like it to relate to it. The rock culture is here to stay, and the question is how best can we appropriate its appeal for the cause of Jesus Christ. With most rock music the message is subordinate to the medium, and that is fortunate, for the message is often profane or obscene. Some would argue that the music itself is demonic, but such an aesthetic judgment is in the ear of the listener, for our response to music as to other forms of art is culturally conditioned. I leave to the theoreticians the solution to the problem of the relationship between the extrinsic and the intrinsic value of the music of modern youth. My interest is in its value to youth evangelism, and my belief is that it can and should be used to reach young people. If that's what young people like, why not? But if it is to have any evangelistic value, the message must be heard. Some evangelists use rock to attract a crowd and then give their message. Others have adapted their message to the medium. There are Christian rock groups, and soft rock is often heard on the programs of the television evangelists. They are way ahead of the churches in relating to this popular musical genre. My point is simply that the pastor-evangelist should not overlook the importance that the youth of today attach to their music. The question is how to make use of rock music in the church without alienating the older generation. Some churches have shown that it can be done.

Their turf. One leaf local churches should borrow from the book of youth ministries like Young Life is the importance of going where the kids are. Too many youth directors in too many churches for too many years have operated on the assumption that all their interaction should take place at the church. Their programs were designed to bring young people to the church, but in so functioning they were not reaching those who didn't respond. Pastors scratched their heads, wondering, "Why don't more kids come out?" They had not learned to go where the kids are! Young Life area directors do that. They show up at the pep rallies, the basketball games, the school plays, the graduation exercises. They know where the kids gather and where they meet to eat. Youth directors and others who want to relate to young people should be willing to mingle with them on their turf. Pastor Jane Smith does not have the time to attend every high school event or to visit with kids in fast food joints and video game parlors, but as an evangelist she will be much more favorably received by the young people she hopes to reach if she visits their turf once in a while. It's a way of showing she cares.

Speaking to Young People

Having identified some of the key plug-in points for relating to young people, I want to address one aspect of youth ministry to which every pastor-evangelist should give serious attention: speaking to youth audiences. Whether it be at a youth conference or a church retreat, a Sunday school rally or a baccalaureate service, a pastor is often called upon to speak to a group of young people. Realizing that public speaking is more of a gift than a skill, more of an art than a science, I should like, nevertheless, to offer some suggestions that can at least help us live up to our God-given potential.

Awareness. You should know as much as you possibly can about the group you have been asked to address. What kind of gathering is it? What is the situation? Why are they there? Why have you been asked to speak and what do they want you to do? How long and how often are you to speak? Will there be other speakers, or are you the only one? If others, what is the theme and how do you fit into it? Try to discover points of identification, points where you can plug into their experience. Acknowledge the areas of disagreement and difficulty, if there are any. You can ask questions to bring these things to the surface. For example, "How many of you are here because you want to be?

How many are here because you have to be? I assume the rest of you don't know why you're here." This lets them know in a humorous way that you realize most of them, at that point anyway, are not very excited about being there.

Flexibility. This is an extremely valuable asset to any speaker. It is related to and dependent upon awareness; that is, a continual awareness of what is going on. The speaker has to be able to read an audience and have a feel for how it's going. Do not be misled by the enthusiasm of some. You have to be ready to adjust to changing moods, circumstances, and needs, not to mention unexpected interruptions. That is when humor can come to the rescue. Speaking to youth is a dynamic exercise. If your canned presentation doesn't pan out, can it! Be flexible.

Style. Develop your own style. Be yourself; don't try to be somebody else. Here are some things to think about.

How to begin. It may be helpful sometimes to begin with an attention-getter, which can be low key (a story or a joke) or high key (something dramatic, noisy, or even shocking). Often your opening will take its cue from the way you are introduced, or from what has happened just before you speak, or from the theme or purpose of the meeting. Let the circumstances determine how you launch into your talk.

Language. By all means use language that communicates, but use it comfortably. Don't fake it. If you misuse the latest jargon, you are in trouble. It is far better not to use it at all than to use it inappropriately.

Humor. The importance of humor in relating to youth has already been discussed. Every speaker should have some funny (preferably original) stories up his or her sleeve and some good one-liners for various occasions. Timing is the key. What makes for good humor is as much in the timing as in the telling. It isn't funny if it's forced, or if it's lost in the laughter of the previous remark. Patience is a virtue in storytelling, as in everything else. The long-remembered Jack Benny and Johnny Carson have shown the world that a pause and a facial expression can be as funny as any joke. The point here is that speakers to youth need to learn how to use humor comfortably and effectively.

Emotion. Be careful here. Emotion is one thing, emotionalism is something else. Young people will respond, as will adults, to genuine emotion. But they can tell the difference between a maudlin imitation and the real thing. Beware the speaker who becomes a spectacle; power to the speaker who can plug into the yearnings, the anxieties, the fears and frustrations, the hopes and joys, the sorrows and affections of young people. The speaker who can relate to the dominant emotions of youth can move an audience spiritually as well as emotionally. How people feel has more to do with their behavior than what people think. To accept Jesus Christ as one's Lord and Savior is an affair of the heart as well as of the mind. How can the awareness of God's presence in one's life not be an emotional experience?

Dialogue. You do well to use a dialogical style when speaking to young people. Interact with your audience, even if you are giving a formal address. You can do this by raising and addressing the questions on the minds of your audience; that is, by verbalizing what they are thinking and speaking to them *as if* they were speaking to you. It is much easier to be dialogical at an informal youth gathering, especially if you can interact with them before your presentation. You can comment positively about them, refer to some of them by name, or tease them good-naturedly. Ask questions that show your interest in who they are and what's happening in their lives. Awareness demands dialogue!

Urgency. As a pastor-evangelist I am no longer content to be merely an entertainer. My days as a would-be comedian are long since over. I want something to happen to the young people I address. I want their lives to change. I don't have time to waste being nothing more than a stand-up comic. I am there to bear witness to Jesus Christ and to challenge young people, as well as adults, to take seriously what it means to be Christ's person in the world today. I may use humor to get their attention, but when I get it they are going to hear about Christ. I may use it to make a point, but the point I want them to remember is Jesus Christ. Just how direct and to what degree that point is made depends upon the audience—who they are and where they are on the ladder of faith. That's why it is so necessary to be aware of your audience and to be flexible!

Content. The pastor-evangelist must also give thought to the content of his or her message to young people. Here are some considerations.

Relate the message to the audience. Some speakers have a canned presentation they are going to lay on their young listeners come hell or high water. To be sure, you should and will have some things you want to say, questions you want to raise, points you want to cover. But you can present them in a way that makes them relevant, vital, and interesting to the group you are addressing. It is not a bad idea to give a rationale for saying what you want to say. Make it relevant—not over their heads but on their level. This does not mean talking down to young people but getting down with them, not lowering yourself to their level but relating to them *at* their level, not trying to be one of them but trying to be one *with* them. To be believable your message must be comprehensible, and to be comprehensible it must be related to their life experience.

Relate the message to the occasion. Make sure the occasion is adequate to the assignment. You can't cover everything. You can't do everything. What is the occasion? What are they expecting you to do, entertain them? Instruct them? Challenge them? Inform them? Inspire them? Remember the point made earlier about the need for awareness; the content of your message should be related to the purpose of your being there and to the occasion. The latter includes the time available to you. What can you do in fifteen minutes? Thirty? An hour? A weekend? What can you accomplish in the time you have? What should you include? What should you omit? Relate the content to the occasion.

Relate the message to your faith. Say what you really believe. It should be something important for your audience because it's important to you. If they're bored, that's their problem; but if you're boring, that's your problem. They are not likely to be bored when you are sharing your faith with sincerity and conviction.

Relate the message to persons. Speak to them as individuals, so that each one feels as if you are speaking directly to him or her. Don't indict or condemn them as a group. Some are this way or that way, but not all. Appeal to their idealism, not their guilt.

The introduction. I cannot stress enough the importance of the introduction—not of your message but of you. How you are introduced probably more than anything else determines how you are received. The introducer's responsibility is to prepare the audience and pave the way for the speaker, but how many fail to do that. They have no sense of the occasion, and don't say the appropriate thing. The introduction should include an enthusiastic statement of why you were asked to be there for this occasion. It does not require a flowery biography, especially if something of that nature has already been distributed in writing or is known to the group. Rather, the audience should hear the introducer's appreciation of and personal relationship to the speaker.

What I am saying applies to introductions not just at youth rallies but at any and all occasions, with any and all audiences. The introducer's role is much more crucial than most people realize, because it is the introduction that largely determines the initial receptivity, even for speakers who are very well known. If the emcee doesn't know the speaker well enough, get someone who does, or at least someone who knows enough about the speaker to present her or him adequately. A good speaker can overcome the handicap of a poor introduction, but for some speakers that is not easy to do. Because most of us, unfortunately, have little control over how we are introduced, the foregoing comments should be seen through the eyes of the introducer, so that we don't do to others what has so often been done to us.

YOUNG ADULTS

What are the unique considerations regarding those whom we call young adults (post–high school through the middle to late twenties)? For the pastor-evangelist the question can be restated: When are young adults likely to be most receptive to the gospel? What opportunities does a pastor have for witnessing to young adults? Some circumstances are common to many in this age group.

Choosing a career. Young men and women sometimes consult their pastor when considering their career. More often, pastors are called upon for a character reference. Such a request affords an excellent opportunity to do some value clarification with the person requesting the reference and to discuss what is really important in his or her life. Those wrestling with a vocational decision are usually receptive to examining goals and priorities in relation to their career possibilities.

Falling in love and marriage. Couples are at their most idealistic during courtship and engagement. They are talking about all kinds of things relating to their life together, sharing their dreams, wanting to build the best possible future for each other. Premarital counseling, therefore, provides a very special faith-sharing opportunity for the pastor-evangelist.

The birth of a child. Young couples who have fallen away from the church are often receptive to the gospel when they have their first child and are confronted with the responsibilities and challenges of parenthood. The miracle of birth sensitizes them to the mystery of life and the sense of awe it evokes. It is a beautiful plug-in point. Hospital visits, prayers with and for the couple, a rose in the pulpit, or an announcement in the church bulletin (if they're members) are all bridges to a renewed awareness of and interest in the church.

Baptism. Closely related to the birth of a child is the decision that one or both of the parents may be facing about their child's baptism. It is a time of serious soul-searching, when they must decide how they want their child to be raised. That decision imposes upon them the need to examine their own relationship to God and the church. It is another golden opportunity for the pastor-evangelist, especially if the young parents are inclined to want their child to be baptized. The prebaptism conference is a time to review with them the covenant story and its significance for their lives and the life of their child.

Divorce and marriage problems. Couples with marital problems often seek help from a pastor. It is a time of great need—for direction, for comfort, for dealing with hostility, anger, guilt, suspicion, jealousy, hurt, anxiety, and many other emotions evoked by the trauma of conflict, separation, or divorce. Often they have no church affiliation or strong religious faith, and the counseling sessions become a pathway back to God for one or both of them.

Family problems. Young couples, like everybody else, have family problems with their own special flavor: the problem of adjustment, when those who have been playing the field must settle down, those who have been free to come and go as they please now are accountable to a spouse or a family, and those who were less worried about their own security now are responsible for or dependent upon the security of others; the problem of relationships with in-laws, establishing one's individuality while honoring others' expectations; the problem of needing privacy and space while having to accept family obligations and impositions; the problem of intergenerational differences and disagreements about how children should be raised; the problem of conflicting loyalties to one's spouse and one's parents; the problems of financial security, of double careers, of religious differences, of clashing moral values. There are enormous pressures on couples these days, and a healthy married life demands a mature commitment and attitude on the part of each spouse.

Singles. Young adults who are single have special needs as well. For some it is a growing anxiety about marriage, as they see their friends getting married and wonder if the right person will ever come along for them. They must come to grips with the possibility of having to remain single. With that comes for some the problem of the conflict between their sexual needs and their religious or moral values. Young divorcées, widows and widowers, and persons who are single by preference all have their special needs, not to mention young adults who are single parents. The church has an important ministry to these persons, in whose lives the pastor as evangelist has a significant part to play. The church is like a spiritual hospital for many people with emotional problems. It is a place for them to come for support and help. In the experience of Christian fellowship, they can rediscover or redefine their identity and get their act together. Young singles in these situations tend to be receptive to the news of a Savior who loves them and a community that cares.

Health problems. Young adults naturally do not have as

many health problems as older people do. That is why it is all the more devastating to their morale when a serious illness develops. Such an experience calls for great courage, strength, and faith. It is a time for the pastor to be available and, as evangelist, to present the good news of a Savior who knows our every need and weakness, who bore a cross before any of us ever did, and whose grace is always sufficient. We bear witness to a God who in everything is able to work for good with those who love him, and from whose love nothing can separate us, not even death itself.

Bereavement. The experience of losing a loved one is for young adults, as for everyone, a time of the greatest receptivity. It may also be a time of great bitterness and guilt. This is all the more reason for a pastor to be available and sensitive to their need and, as an evangelist, to speak the appropriate word of faith at the appropriate time.

Other considerations. There are many other circumstances that affect young adults along with others, including economic reversals, unemployment, setbacks and failures of various kinds, and such natural disasters as fires and floods. The situations I have listed are not unique to younger people but affect them either more frequently or in a special way. They are opportune times for the pastor to do the work of an evangelist.

But how to go about it? We can draw a few hints from what has already been said. I have found the best approach with young adults is to plug into their possibilities: their aspirations, their worthy desires, their worth and strengths as persons. I try to help them put their problems into perspective, identify and consider the alternatives, and become excited about new beginnings and new goals. In most situations there is a need to clarify values, reorder priorities, restate objectives, and recommit to one's highest ideals, best dreams, and brightest hopes. These are times to question their idols and to take a good look at the one person worthy of their total commitment, loyalty, and love, who can help them be their best selves, who expects the best of them, wants the best for them, and gives the best to them—Jesus Christ. Most young adults have not lost the idealism of youth. Plug into it!

MIDDLE-AGED PERSONS

Many of the same situations pertain to persons in the nebulous period called middle age. The Middle Ages are referred to as the Dark Ages of human history. For some the middle years are dark years indeed, a time of disillusionment and despair, of fading hopes and vanished dreams, a time when the ambitions of young adulthood are finally discarded and the painful necessity of accepting one's limitations is realized. Middle-aged women and men have their own kinds of problems.

Caring for aging parents. This is terribly difficult for many a middle-aged son or daughter, who may not have the financial resources to provide permanent nursing care or the space, physical stamina, or willing cooperation of a spouse to accommodate and care for an ailing and aging parent. The guilt engendered by having to put their parent in a nursing home, the worry and inconvenience of living too far away to be as available and helpful as they would like to be, the resentment caused by the unwillingness of a sister or brother to share the burden, the anxiety of dwindling finances and an uncertain future—these are all too common problems for middle-aged sons and daughters. And the situation is worsening, as people's life expectancy increases. In my experience, this has been one of the most difficult and prevalent problems. In their desperation, families often have nowhere to turn for help except to their church.

Readjustment. As their children grow up and leave the nest, parents have the challenge of discovering each other all over again and rebuilding their married life around each other, instead of around their children. It's back to basics, back to square one—the way it was when they started out. Yet it's not the same, because it's twenty or twenty-five years later. The challenge is also an opportunity, and the pastor-evangelist can help couples in this transition period to see the possibilities for a wonderful new dimension of life, one that is built on the foundation of a memory-filled relationship.

Loneliness. Middle-aged single persons have their special needs too. They may have come to enjoy their independence, but they have also begun to realize their aloneness. Single persons have to work harder to keep their friends, especially their married friends. They wonder who will notice their absence when they're missing or care for them when they're sick, or remember them when they're gone. They need a family, someone to belong to, a support group of friends who care. The church can be that family, that support group, that remembering community. The pastor-evangelist should help them to recognize and want that.

Self-doubt. This is a syndrome of middle age, when men and women may begin to question their life's vocation and wonder if they made the right choice of careers. This is also the time when they are especially vulnerable to an extramarital affair, for they wonder if they've lost their sex appeal. They are particularly susceptible to the wiles of some attractive person of the opposite sex who cares not a hoot about breaking up a marriage. On the contrary, that makes it all the more interesting and exciting! So "harmless" flirtations become affairs, and affairs become romances, and romances lead to divorces, and divorces pave the way for second marriages. The circumstances may differ, but the pattern is the same. For the pastor it is an evangelistic opportunity to help both the "cheater" and the "cheated."

Impending old age. Many middle-aged persons find this reality difficult to accept. Some dread the thought of retirement and the uncertainties of a changing life-style. The prospect of growing old is depressing for many and frightening for some. They would like to be nearer to their children, but they don't want to be a burden to them. They wonder if their retirement income will be sufficient, and they worry about their health, as more and more of their friends and acquaintances suffer strokes and heart attacks.

Once again, in relating to persons in their middle years the pastor as evangelist should plug into their point of need. The church can help with many of the problems that middle-aged people have. Offer assistance to those who need help finding a nursing home or some kind of retirement community for their parents. Have a network of agencies to whom you can refer families for help. If the need is for a sense of self-worth, help them to understand how God values persons: not by their worldly success or material possessions but by their faith in God and their love for others. The church is one community where people are judged not by what they have but by what they are, not by their position but by their discipleship.

If the need is for readjustment, help them to discover the joy of belonging to and participating in a family of faith. We are not alone. We belong to a fellowship that transcends all human barriers, including even death, for the family of faith will be here long after you and I have been buried in the dust of the earth. The members of the family come and go, but the family remains. The faces in the pews will be different a hundred years from now, but it's the same family—and the same faith.

OLDER PEOPLE

When is a person old? There are many answers to that question. Some say you are as old as you feel. Others say old age begins when you start lying about it—or when you think you have to hide it! Some people seem old when they're fifty and others seem young when they're eighty. Aging is as much a matter of the spirit as of the flesh. When people are young in spirit, you don't think of them as old. There have been some amazing octogenarians in every church I have served, persons who seemed to have found the secret of eternal youth. They were so young in spirit that I never thought of them as old.

Concerns of the Elderly

Old age is a reality—inevitable, if you live long enough! Father Time takes his toll, and those of whom he exacts it have their special problems and needs, in addition to the kinds that are shared by all people.

Finances. Older people are often worried about their financial security, especially those who are on fixed incomes and have to deal with inflation. "How long can I afford to live where I am now? Will I have enough money to sustain me through a long illness? Can I afford to go into a retirement home? What if they turn our apartment house into a condominium? What if they keep raising the rent?" These are worrisome questions for older folks.

Health. Related to financial worries is the anxiety about impending health problems, culminating perhaps in a long terminal illness. That final illness or sudden attack comes to us all, unless we die in an accident or of unnatural causes. No one looks forward to being hospitalized or to being confined to a nursing home. The thought of becoming an invalid or of being totally dependent or senile, and the indignity of being in such a state, is horribly depressing.

Loneliness. So is the loneliness that is the partner of old age. The longer you live, the more loved ones and friends you lose. And every death seems harder to bear than the last. When you are young and mobile, you don't realize what it is like to be alone. Old people long for friends. They cherish every minute with a loved one, and they read every piece of mail their eyes can see. They appreciate every little favor—a phone call, a card, a visit from a friend. The church ought to be that friend.

Death. Then there is the reality of their own death, a reality many people are unwilling or unable to face. They know it is inevitable, but they can't talk about it. The pastor as evangelist can help them to accept that reality, and deal with it, and plan for it, and transcend it! Who more than the person who takes death seriously should be ready for the message of eternal life?

Uselessness. Even before the period of total dependence there is a time when older folks may feel useless, unneeded and unwanted. It is very important for older people, like everyone else, to feel they have something to contribute. It is in the community of faith that their self-worth is affirmed and their lives can find purpose and meaning.

Frustration. Closely related to the feeling of uselessness is the frustration that many older persons experience, as they think back over their lives: so many unfulfilled ambitions, so many unrealized goals, so many disappointments. The pastor-evangelist can help those who feel this way to see themselves not as failures but as interesting and worthwhile human beings, whom God loves and values and who are judged not by their failures and successes but by the sincerity of their faith.

Relating to Older People

Some pastors relate better to senior citizens than to youth. But there are also pastors who have not discovered how interesting and enjoyable an elderly person can be. Here are some things for the pastor-evangelist to keep in mind.

Love them! The best way to learn to appreciate older people is to get to know them. When you know them, you'll love them; when you love them, you'll overlook their idiosyncrasies, just as they'll overlook yours. Relate to them individually, not collectively; as persons, not as objects; as sensitive human beings, not as unfeeling relics.

Listen to them! They need someone to listen, especially if they are alone or lonely. Hear them out. Let them talk about their past, share their experiences, express their views. They like and need to feel that someone is interested in what they have to say and appreciates what they have to contribute.

Learn from them! They have much to teach us. They have mellowed with the years. Their hearts are scarred with the experiences of pain and grief. They have been tested in the crucible of suffering and have learned about life the hard way —by living it. Older folks can tell us many things, if we will only listen. And in the sharing of their lives with us, they find a new joy in living.

Share the gospel! They are ready to hear it. Give them hope. The gospel speaks to their needs. Ask them to share their faith, which you will find they readily do, when asked. After they have been reminiscing a bit, you might say, "What part has your faith played in these experiences?" Or, "You mentioned not being around for another Christmas. If you really think you might die before then, are you ready for it?" Or, "How do you feel about God, Roberta?" Listen for plug-in points and, when the time is right, share your own faith, relating your faith story to the other person's story and showing how both relate to *the* story.[52]

Show the gospel! Here is where the church as the community of faith is so important, for its members serve God by helping people. The program of a servant church should be geared to meet the needs of those both inside and outside its walls. Here are some things a church can do for older people, so that the gospel we share may show in our deeds.

Retirement age council. Have some sort of council to address the concerns and needs of the older people in the church and in the community. Its membership should not be limited to older people but should be broadly representative, in order to be able to plan and implement a varied program of activities and events for senior citizens, including seminars on subjects of interest to older people (estate planning, dealing with Medicare, retirement tips, etc.).

Spiritual activities. Older people enjoy participating in Bible study and prayer groups and other inspirational events, along with everyone else. An effort should be made to see that they are able to attend these activities at church as often as they like. Sometimes the pastor or members of the church conduct services or Bible studies for those in nursing homes.

Service activities. Think of things for the older members to do to feel useful and wanted. If their health permits, they can serve as telephone volunteers and receptionists, stuff envelopes, and make telephone calls. They may need transportation in order to take part in some church event or activity. Find out their interests and call upon their experience and expertise. Ask their opinions, involve them in the decision-making process, and, if they are mobile, invite them to serve on committees and in the organizations of the church. Even shut-ins can have a ministry; they can be part of your prayer network or your telephone calling team. I think of an elderly blind man in a wheelchair who every day would call five shut-ins like himself and visit and pray with them on the telephone. That was his ministry and his joy.

Fellowship activities. The possibilities are unlimited: arts and crafts, parties, dances, sewing groups, folk dancing, songfests, speakers, church suppers, picnics, sightseeing tours, and on and on. These should be open to senior citizens in the community at large, who in the warmth and friendliness of Christian fellowship may become interested in joining the church. The pastor as evangelist is always alert to that possibility.

Recognition dinner. Have an annual recognition dinner for longtime members of the church. Provide transportation for shut-ins and those who otherwise could not attend. Honor the oldest and recognize them all. Plan an interesting and fun-filled program, with an opportunity for these members to make any comments they care to.

Transportation needs. Transportation can be a major problem for shut-ins and people who are no longer able to drive. There should be a transportation committee to see to the needs of such persons, not just to bring them to church but to drive them to the market, or to a doctor's appointment, or just on an outing. If the need warrants it and the church can afford it, a van or a minibus might be a good investment.

Calling. Visiting shut-ins and the elderly is extremely important and much appreciated by those called upon. Lay callers should be trained for the task, to be sure they are sensitive to any needs they encounter and are able to listen and relate to those they visit. They should be comfortable about reading the scripture and offering prayer, both of which are meaningful and beneficial to shut-ins.

Tape recordings. Cassette recordings of the worship services can be made available for those who are unable to come to church. Machines that play cassette tapes (but do not record) are very easy to operate. They can be left at the home and picked up later, so that the shut-in or sick person can listen at his or her leisure. Be selective in the use of the tapes, as some messages may be more appropriate than others. It is considerate to edit the tape down to no more than thirty minutes, as an hour of listening might be tiring for a sick person. It may be just a particular anthem or solo that you want the person to hear. This is a worthy undertaking for whatever group is responsible for the ministry of compassion in your church.

Printed sermons. Copies of the sermons can be mimeographed and distributed to those who want them and will read them. Pastors who do this hear regularly from some of the recipients and occasionally from others. That correspondence is important, for it makes people feel closer to the church and to their pastor. Moreover, the printed sermons are often shared with friends and relatives.

Flowers. Most churches distribute the chancel flowers to

those who are sick at home or in the hospital and to other elderly persons, especially shut-ins or partial shut-ins. The typical church bouquet can be divided easily into three or four smaller bunches, which, if they are delivered Sunday afternoon, will still look fresh. It is a good idea to include a copy of the bulletin from the service that morning or a card with a little message.

Greeting cards. Birthday cards are another way of remembering older persons. If you have time, a handwritten note is an added touch. There are other occasions, such as wedding anniversaries, when a card or a note is a thoughtful way to show you care.

Communion. Serving Communion to shut-ins is another important part of your pastoral ministry. When done on the same day the sacrament is observed in church, it underscores in a beautiful way the unity of the body of Christ and the fellowship of the household of faith.

Youth groups. Young people usually relate well to older folks. They are uninhibited about touching and hugging, and they convey a joyful, caring spirit. Involve your youth group in a ministry to the elderly, and both groups will find it rewarding. The friendships that result are important for young and old alike. Caroling at Christmastime, delivering tape recordings of the services, taking the flowers or baskets of food, and doing various household chores are some of the ways young people can be involved. One youth group I know about offers their services to the older folks by announcing, "We are your slaves for the day. We're yours to command!"

Other services. The official boards and other organizations of the church can provide many other services to help meet the physical and personal needs of older members and nonmembers, especially those who have no family to look after them. The pastor-evangelist should be giving inspirational leadership to this effort, which is part of the church's *service* evangelism.

In this chapter I have attempted to identify and discuss briefly some of the factors relating to five different age categories, which factors must be kept in mind by the pastor-evangelist in ministering to persons in those categories. We turn next to another important consideration, the question of number.

8

The Pastor's Contextual Considerations: Number

The number of persons to whom the pastor-evangelist is relating is a second factor to consider. You don't speak to a couple in their living room the way you speak to a congregation from the pulpit. Living room sermons are about as appropriate as a tuxedo at a picnic. Relating to a person one-on-one is vastly different from speaking to a congregation of five hundred, or a class of thirty, or a group of six.

GENERAL PRINCIPLES

No matter how many or how few persons are involved, however, some general principles apply.

Direction. Whenever you are evangelizing, you should have a clear sense of direction. What are you trying to accomplish? Whether it be one person or many to whom you are bearing witness, you should keep your goals clearly in mind.

Awareness. With individuals as with groups, it is important to know to whom you are witnessing. Be your audience many or few, the more you know about them the better you can relate to them. Read them carefully, and keep reading them to note any changes that occur in the dynamic relationship you have established with them. Awareness is the key to relevance.

Flexibility. This is an essential quality for good communicators. It means being able to ride with the punches, to adjust to the unexpected, to react appropriately rather than overreact to what's happening.

Sensitivity. Flexibility, in turn, requires sensitivity, the ability to read people's facial expressions and body language. This is as true for public speaking as it is for interpersonal witnessing. The sensitive communicator knows "what's going on" as well as "what's happening."

Consistency. The approach will vary with the target, but the evangelist's style should be consistent. That means be yourself, wherever you are—be it at a Kiwanis luncheon or on a youth retreat. Being consistent does not mean sticking to one method but following one Lord. Be consistent in what you stand for, what you believe in, and how you live your faith. Be consistent in word and deed. Nothing destroys one's credibility faster than actions that deny one's words.

NUMERICAL IMPLICATIONS

Having mentioned a few general rules that apply regardless of the number of persons involved, let me now suggest some of the distinctions of which the pastor-evangelist should be aware in relating to different numbers of people.

Large audiences. These designations are confessedly arbitrary. For the purpose of this discussion, a large audience means two hundred or more persons.

One-way dialogue. You can't converse with two hundred persons. You therefore have to accomplish your desire to be dialogical by the style of your presentation—by raising and addressing their questions and speaking their thoughts for them. If you have time at the end, you can invite questions from the audience. The danger here is that the questions will not be relevant to the group or to your presentation. For that reason, some speakers like to have questions submitted in writing, so they can select the most pertinent ones.

Volume. As a general rule, the larger the audience the more dramatic you can be. You don't want to sound as if you are addressing a political party convention when you're speaking to a communicants class of three. Histrionics belong on the stage. The smaller the group the more conversational your tone can be, with fewer inflections, softer emphasis, and more breaks in your thought patterns. With large audiences, on the other hand, you can orate—if that's your style. In any case, make sure you can be heard, especially if there is no public-address system. Direct your remarks to the people in the rear.

Participation. Audience participation has to be more carefully controlled when you are speaking to large numbers of people. The larger the number the more unwieldy the physical movement, for instance. Hence, any physical activity you ask them to do should be something they can do easily, such as clapping or raising hands, rising, or turning in place and greeting the persons next to them. To suggest to a thousand people seated in an auditorium that they go find someone with the same initials and share their faith story for five minutes with that person would be to invite pandemonium.

Response. An evangelist should always give his or her hearers an appropriate way to respond. But remember, the larger the audience the more persons there are who may not be "with it." They can be made to feel left out—or, what is even worse, manipulated—by an insensitive, overeager evangelist who assumes everyone either is eager to jump up and come forward or is totally comfortable with seeing others jump up and come forward, when the invitation is given. Read your audience well, so that your appeal allows people to respond to whatever degree and at whatever level they can.

The introduction. Unless you are an international or a national celebrity, the larger the audience the more people there are who don't know you or why you're there, and the less intimate will be your contact with most of them. For this reason, and for the others mentioned in Chapter 7, the introduction of the person who will address a large audience is exceedingly important.

Anonymity. The larger the audience the greater the anonymity of its members. It's easier to hide in a crowd. Those attending a mass youth rally or a worship service in a large church do not know everybody or perhaps even *anybody* else. They may want to be alone in the crowd and may resent any invasion of their anonymity, or they may feel left out. Instead of assuming that a spirit of togetherness prevails, the sensitive evangelist will speak to the audience as individuals, allowing each one to relate to the message wherever he or she is at the moment.

Intimacy. The larger the audience the farther removed the speaker will be from most people. You have to compensate for that distance by your manner of speaking, which should be relational, personal, friendly, and warm. In a small group you have the advantage of face and body language, whereas with a large audience many people may not be able to see what you look like. The people in the back of the auditorium or sitting in a 60,000-seat stadium cannot see your facial expressions (unless your face is displayed on a huge video screen). You have to compensate for the distance between you and your audience, therefore, by what you say and how you say it.

Music. The larger the audience the more useful music becomes, including group singing. You don't usually invite a couple to sing when you're alone with them in their living room. ("I think it's time for a hymn, friends. Would you join me in a stanza of 'Day Is Dying in the West'? You don't know that one? How about, 'Nearer, My God, to Thee'? You would rather I sing it alone?")

Medium-size audiences. I have in mind audiences of seventy-five to two hundred people. With groups of this size dialogue is easier, though it must still be controlled; intimacy is aided by better visibility, which allows face language and body language to reinforce verbal communication; group activities are easier to manage, if there is sufficient space; the need to orate is slightly less. You should not sound to a group of eighty worshipers as if you were announcing the winner of a championship boxing match at Madison Square Garden or delivering an address on the steps of the Lincoln Memorial to 100,000 people at a peace rally. With a medium-size audience you can be more direct and personal, less formal and oratorical. Suit your volume to the hearers. Music is still very important, and as with groups of any size it should be sensitive to their tastes and appropriate to the occasion, so that it enhances and augments rather than detracts from the message.

Small audiences. This would be an audience of more than thirty but under seventy-five persons. Remember, these are arbitrary designations; please do not hold me too rigidly to them. What I have come to know from experience is that the dynamics vary with the size of the group, and I am simply attempting to point out the implications of the numerical variations for the public speaker, in this case the pastor-evangelist. With smaller audiences dialogue is obviously going to be even easier, intimacy even greater, group activities even easier to control, and the need for histrionics even less. You don't orate to the thirty members of the Golden Age Club who invite you to be their luncheon speaker at the YMHA. When you overdo it, you've overdone it! If you become too theatrical, you become a performer instead of a communicator, an actor instead of a witness. If a clever performer is what you want to be, then go to it. But an evangelist should be more interested in people's getting the message than in their being impressed by a performance. Pastor-evangelists should be more concerned about how the message gets through than about how they come across.

Large groups. I am referring to a gathering of twenty to twenty-nine persons. You may be making a speech, directing a workshop, conducting a seminar, or leading a retreat. The demands on the speaker or leader will vary according to the nature and purpose of the group, but in terms of numbers you should recognize that the dynamics of a large group are quite different from those of a small group or of any audience. I never think of a group of twenty persons as an audience, even if I am making a formal presentation. They are a group or gathering of individuals with whom I want to interrelate and with whom I hope to accomplish certain objectives. Usually these have been identified and agreed upon beforehand. If it is to be a one-time presentation with no preliminary interaction, I like to take a little time at the start of my talk to get a feel for where they are. An evangelist needs to be sensitive to the various moods, concerns, and expectations represented in the group and to work hard at involving all the participants, not just the few unrestrained spirits who would do all the talking if you let them. It is harder to remain anonymous in a group of twenty-five people, but it is possible to be a silent partner, or just an observer, instead of a participant. The perceptive leader can read the face

language for clues to how things are going and use the break
periods for seeking out persons who may have something on
their mind.

Medium-size groups. Eleven to nineteen persons would constitute a medium-size group, by my definition. The smaller the
group the greater the intimacy. It is also easier in smaller groups
for the leader to facilitate participation, and harder for the
members to avoid it. Because the group is smaller, the members
can sit closer to each other; because they are physically closer,
they can see each other better. That is a significant factor in
interpersonal communication. People communicate better when
they can look into each other's eyes and talk face to face. Some
people like to sit on the fringes of large groups and even medium-size groups. They seem to want a way out, an escape route.
The observer role is easier to assume. The pastor as evangelist
should help the group members to relate to each other, as well
as to Christ. In other words, help the group to become a group!

Small groups. We are now talking about three to ten persons.
In such a group the dominant desire is to belong. The fear is not
being unable to get out but rather being left out. The person on
the fringe (outside the circle) feels apart from the group. In
small groups you want everyone to be in the circle, as close
together as you comfortably can get. Dialogue replaces mono-
logue, and the leader becomes a facilitator rather than a domina-
tor of discussion, a listener rather than a lecturer, more of a
witness than a proclaimer. The dynamics of a small group are
low-key yet intense, sensitive yet direct, confessional yet confi-
dential, relational yet at times confrontational, open yet exclusive. The pastor as evangelist can invite responses much more
directly. Feelings can be expressed more freely. Prayers are
shared more readily. Intimacy is more easily attained. Whereas
you stand on a platform to speak to an audience, you lead a
small group discussion sitting down. I have found that a unified
response is easier to achieve with a small group than with a
larger one, for the leader has a greater opportunity to help the
participants to interrelate and to promote a spirit of unity.
Affirm them, encourage them, look for the elements of truth in
what they have to say, remind them of their need to be honest

about their feelings, and help them to listen sympathetically and to relate positively to one another. In group discussions the pastor-evangelist is constantly trying to focus the questions and help the group to think theologically. Remember that even if there are only a few persons present, it is still a group, and when you focus on one person, you will find some or perhaps all of the others assuming the role of observers. The task is to relate to the group in such a way that each person responds to Christ individually, positively, and above all personally.

Two persons. Two persons are not a group. The dynamics vary according to their relationship with each other and with you, their spiritual receptivity, the purpose of your being together, the context and setting of the meeting, and many other factors, all of which call for the pastor-evangelist's best interpersonal witnessing skills. If the two persons are emotionally and spiritually compatible, your approach to them is quite different from what it would be if they are at odds with each other. In the latter case the pastor as evangelist must avoid the temptation to relate only to the more receptive person, lest the other become even more alienated. You would instead alternate between the two, directing your attention back and forth, asking sensitive questions, pointing out what is reasonable, and acting as a mediator when it is helpful and appropriate to do so. As a caring listener you hope to win the trust of and establish a relationship with each of them, so that each is free to make his or her decision. If one person becomes a spectator, the task of witnessing to the other is exasperatingly complex and difficult. If there are three people present it had better be a three-way conversation, or your faith sharing may be lost on the silent partner. The other danger is that the one to whom you are relating may become self-conscious and overly aware of the other person's spectator role. These comments are intended to underscore the need for the pastor-evangelist to be sensitive to the dynamics of the situation. It goes without saying that face language and body language are tremendously important in these situations.

One person. The heart of evangelism is one person telling another person about Jesus Christ. Evangelism is interpersonal communication, and the basic level of interpersonal communication is one-to-one. The pastor as evangelist ought to be comfortable in this situation, but as our survey shows (see Chapter 1), many are not. In the workshops and seminars I conduct, there are always some who admit that one of the hardest things for them to do is to share their faith with another person, one-on-one. The reason for this, I am convinced, is that they have never thought through the *why* of their own faith, pursuing the question to its ultimate conclusion. They have not wrestled enough with the paradox of the gift and the grasp or taken seriously the givenness of their faith. That observation is intended not as a put-down but as a challenge to those who balk at interpersonal witnessing to rethink their own faith. That is the starting point for all evangelists.

It goes without saying that one-to-one witnessing is the most intimate, direct, and personal form of evangelism. Because there is only one other person involved, it is also the least complex, in terms not of the content of the message but of the context of the encounter. The two persons are able to concentrate on each other without the distraction of a spectator or the complications that increase in geometric proportion to the number of persons involved. The greater degree of privacy mitigates self-consciousness and facilitates the trusting relationship that is so essential to faith sharing.

It is difficult and somewhat artificial to isolate, as I have been attempting to do, a single factor among the many elements that define the context of evangelism. Each factor must be understood in relation to all the others. It is necessary, nevertheless, to separate them in order to discuss them in some orderly way. In this chapter we have been concentrating on number, which, as we have seen, has obvious implications for one's evangelistic approach. With regard to one-to-one evangelism, much more needs to be said about an appropriate *style* of interpersonal communication. Since that subject has implications beyond the scope of this chapter, I shall address it separately, after having considered some other important contextual factors.

9

The Pastor's Contextual Considerations: The Medium

Another factor that helps define the context for evangelism is the medium by which the message is conveyed. It makes a difference whether one is talking on the telephone or on television. What are some of the differences, and what are the implications for evangelism?

CORRESPONDENCE

I begin with what may well be the most frequently yet ineffectively used medium for evangelism. Correspondence is an indispensable means of exercising pastoral care and a readily available channel for communicating the gospel. The pastor-evangelist should give thought to the challenge and the opportunity that this medium presents. What is a Christian letter? It is not just a letter written by a Christian! Rather, it is a letter with a Christian message or tone, one that addresses a problem or need from a Christian perspective. A Christian letter comes from the sender in the name of or in the spirit of Jesus Christ.

When one is evangelistically sensitive, however, one has to take into consideration the recipient or recipients of the letter, or else one's evangelistic language may create a gap between the writer and the recipient. Pastors find themselves having to write all kinds of letters—sympathy notes; letters of recommendation or congratulations; replies to questions of all kinds; letters to the lost, the lonely, and the lovelorn; and letters to those wrestling with major decisions, problems, worries, or fears; not to mention business letters, congregational letters, appeal letters, thank-you letters, and many, many other kinds. Remembering that letters you write may be the kind people want as keepsakes, you would do well to take a look at this medium through evangelistic glasses. Here are some thoughts about some of the more frequent kinds of letters.

Sympathy letters. When someone you know dies, or a relative of someone you know, you may want to write a note of sympathy or comfort to the bereaved, sometimes in lieu of and sometimes in addition to your being with the family in person. While every letter is individualized to suit the situation, there are some general principles to keep in mind.

Write notes. Handwritten sympathy notes mean more to people than typewritten letters. How many times I have received appreciative comments from persons to whom I have sent a note or letter in my own handwriting. Such notes are more personal, because they were not dictated. They are right from the heart to the page. And because they take longer, they are appreciated all the more by people who know how busy a pastor can be.

Use scripture. It has its own healing power! But use it appropriately. The Bible can say some things much better than we can, and people are usually more receptive to the gospel in time of bereavement.

Invite sharing. Invite the persons to whom you write to share their feelings with you. That is therapeutic for the bereaved, who welcome the opportunity to express their thoughts about their loved one in writing to a caring pastor.

Don't minimize. Don't give easy or trite answers to the mystery of death, or minimize the reality of suffering and grief. Job had no answer for the *why* of suffering, and neither do we. But we do know that nothing can separate us from the love of God, which is in Christ Jesus our Lord.

Don't pretend. Even if you have experienced such a loss, do you really know how another person feels when a loved one dies? Only God knows the depth of our private pain. You can empathize, but don't pretend. Don't say "I know how you feel" and then tell them how they ought to feel. The person who is experiencing the anguish of losing a loved one may feel that *nobody* can understand.

Offer something. If you can, offer something specific. "Would you like me to arrange transportation to church for you?" is better than "Let me know if I can ever be of help." They almost never let you know!

Congratulatory letters. Just as we remind people of God's presence in time of trouble, so we remind them of God's goodness in time of celebration. You don't do this by exhorting them to give God the credit for their accomplishments but by rejoicing with them or for them in the evidence of God's gracious gifts. You do it as an expression of your own faith rather than as an appeal to their faith. For example, "I thank God for you, Michael, and for giving you the talent to win the skating championship," or for whatever it is Michael has just accomplished. Or, "What a great God—one who not only gives you this amazing ability but who can inspire and enable all of us to use whatever talents we are given!" That is better than saying, "Before you finish reading another word of this letter, Clarence, you ought to get down on your knees and thank God for letting your team win!" Affirm the other person, share your joy in his or her success, express your pride in his or her accomplishments, and praise the God who is the source of all blessings.

Letters of advice. In the medium of correspondence, as in other forms of counseling, be careful about being too directive or prescriptive. Your printed words of wisdom might not seem so relevant or applicable down the road a piece. Encourage the recipient to seek the help of a God who is ready, willing, and able to help those who turn to God for the wisdom and guidance that only God can provide, who in everything works for good with those who love God and are called according to God's purpose, and who is merciful and forgiving, when our best efforts to discern and do God's will are frustrated by the limitations of our own humanity.

Thank-you letters. Express your thanks in the context of your faith. "I thank God for a friend like you," or "Your letter was a gift from God, Marion, an answer to prayer," or "What you did reminded me once more of the marvelous ways God works through people to work the miracles of grace."

Friend-to-friend letters. Let the person know who gets the credit for the good things that happen to you and who is your strength, comfort, and hope in time of trouble. But it is better to do it in a low-key fashion. A sensitive evangelist does not want to overpower the reader any more than a person he or she is evangelizing face to face. Invite a faith response, share a faith insight, suggest a faith possibility.

Christmas letters. Ann Landers' aversion to them notwithstanding, my wife and I enjoy receiving and sending Christmas letters. For many years our Christmas letter has been our Christmas greeting, in lieu of sending cards. It is a way of keeping in touch with many friends who otherwise would never hear from us. The question is, How do you make your witness, when some of your friends are Christians, some are adherents of other faiths, and some are unbelievers or whatever? You either have to write separate letters to your Christian friends and your non-Christian friends or you have to write a letter that is appropriate for all. You would not, for example, address such a letter, "Dear Christian Friends" or "Dear Friends in Christ," and you would not (or should not) sign it, "Your friend in Christ." Share your faith in God, but do not *overdo* it. Aim for the highest common denominator and build upon that. Your faith comes through in the way you deal with the events of your life, your tragedies and triumphs. Your non-Christian friends have no right to object and will not object to your saying how you feel about things. What they are likely to object to is your addressing them as if your feelings are *their* feelings.

Letters in general. Here are some dos and don'ts for letter writing in general.

Don't overdo it. Try not to sound like Holy Harriet or Pious Pete. Use evangelical language sparingly and judiciously, especially if the recipient is not a Christian.

Don't underdo it. Some people would never know we are Christians by our letters. We should not impose our faith, but we need not hide it, and we surely should not apologize for it.

Don't presume. Don't address someone as a believer if he or she is not. And don't close with "Sincerely in Christ" or some similar closing, if the other person is not a Christian.

Do use scripture. But use it judiciously, correctly, and comfortably. By judiciously, I mean with sensitivity about how it will be received and understood by the person to whom you are writing; by correctly, I mean with biblical and theological integrity; by comfortably, I mean not to instruct but to inspire, not to sound "religious" but to appeal to faith, not artificially to haul in a proof text, but sincerely to share verses that have shaped your faith.

Do think about to whom you are writing. Gear your witness to the person. If you know he or she is not a Christian, or if you are not sure, it would still be appropriate to share your own faith, or some biblical truth or insight, or a thought or experience that was meaningful for you. Sometimes you may even want to suggest a possibility or invite a response, but do it sensitively.

Do pray! Undergird whatever you do with prayer. The God who inspires your preaching can also inspire your letter writing.

THE TELEPHONE

Until the day when the telecommunications industry has made electronic audiovisual conversation available to and affordable for all people, the telephone remains the most effective medium for interpersonal dialogue. It is the next best thing to face-to-face conversation. Despite the huge amount of time most pastors spend on the telephone, one wonders how much of our conversation bears witness to our faith in Jesus Christ. Here are some suggestions for the pastor-evangelist who would like to baptize this medium.

Vocal compensation. In a telephone conversation your voice is the only thing to which the other person can respond. The person at the other end of the line cannot see your face and body language. He or she does not know if you are smiling or frowning. To come across as friendly, you have to *sound* friendly. To come across as interested, you have to *sound* interested. To come across as caring, you have to *sound* as if you care. Your voice has to compensate for what your face and body cannot communicate. I call this the rule of vocal compensation.

Auditory accommodation. The absence of visual contact works both ways. Since you cannot see the other person, you have to listen all the more carefully. Because it is more difficult to hear when both people are speaking at once, you have to give the other person more opportunities to break in, and be more careful yourself not to interrupt. All the rules of interpersonal witnessing apply. The only difference is that since your eyes cannot help you, you have to rely on your sense of hearing. I call this the rule of auditory accommodation.

Telephonic inspiration. A telephone call is sometimes a convenient and often a necessary substitute for being there in person, especially where distance is a factor. That is all the more reason for the pastor-evangelist to want the telephone conversation to be as meaningful and as helpful as possible. I have found that it is as easy to have a faith-sharing conversation on the telephone as it is in person. I discovered long ago that the telephone is a marvelous medium for prayer, and it is amazing how close two people can feel to each other and to God when they do pray together on the telephone. It is as if someone were whispering a prayer into your ear and direct to your heart, as the human voice and the Holy Spirit transcend the distance that separates you. The very absence of visual and tactile contact heightens the spiritual impact. That is what I mean by telephonic inspiration.

RADIO

The vocal compensation rule applies also to the medium of radio, except that on the radio you are speaking to an unknown audience. Many pastors would do well to listen to and learn from the professionals. Radio announcers do not read commercials as people normally speak. They are much more animated —in tone, pitch, rate, and emphasis. Disc jockeys are the prime examples—too much so for me, but not for their usual audiences. They serve to make the point: You have to compensate vocally for the lack of visual identification. If radio announcers did commercials the way some members of the clergy address an interfaith panel discussion, they wouldn't sell much toothpaste!

Apart from the broadcasting of their religious services, there are many opportunities for pastors to be on the radio. They are asked to do one-minute meditations and five-minute sign-offs, spot prayers and interviews, interfaith panels and ecumenical talks, and many other kinds of shows. I remember appearing as a guest on a late-night talk show in Philadelphia hosted by a widely known character who reveled in controversy. I had been ordained just two weeks before, and this was the first time I had ever had to defend the faith on the air for two hours. The challenge presented by my ungenial host would have been difficult enough without the constant interruptions from the listeners, most of whom seemed to have an ax to grind with organized religion. It was my baptism by fire!

A Christian friend who happened to hear the broadcast that night commented to me later that I was not evangelical enough in my witness. He might have been right, although my Jewish host would not have agreed with him. Judging from the questions of the listeners, many in the radio audience would have turned off and tuned out had I come on too strong. The fans of that show were not eager to hear a radio preacher. I was trying to reach them where they were and to communicate the gospel in terms they could understand. My friend was playing a different language game.

That was long before I had thought through my own theology and methodology of evangelism. Now I am more convinced than ever that too many evangelical Christians spend too much time talking to each other in the language they know and not enough time talking to the world in language the world can understand. It may be too strong an indictment, but I would have to say that most of the preaching I hear on radio and television is not evangelistically sensitive, because it is directed only or mostly to Christians. So the unbelieving world doesn't get the message, because the case is never made. The gospel must be preached in terms the world can understand!

The problem is partly due to the fact that much religious programming is devoted to the broadcasting of church services. What the radio audience is doing in effect, therefore, is eavesdropping on some congregation in the act of worship. The *evangelistic* value of such broadcasts is questionable, simply because the services are designed for a worshiping congregation, a family of faith, not for unbelievers. There has to be much more awareness of and sensitivity to the radio audience than are reflected in the broadcast of most church services.

With these preliminary thoughts in mind, here are some guidelines for using the medium of radio.

Be sensitive to the unbelievers. Don't assume that everyone out there is a Christian. Be sensitive to the unchurched and the unbelievers who may be listening.

Watch your language. It is not a captive audience. Avoid the jargon that causes non-Christians to tune out before they hear the whole message. You have to capture and hold their interest; they don't have to stay with you till the end of the service.

Watch your attitude. Avoid making statements that communicate arrogance, intolerance, narrow-mindedness, or naiveté. Such statements reinforce the negative impressions that church antagonists have of preachers.

Have a two-pronged approach. When broadcasting a worship service, keep in mind that there are two audiences, the congregation and the radio listeners. You must maintain a balance between the two. Bring the radio audience into the church by speaking to them directly at times, explaining what is happening (they don't have a printed bulletin), avoiding awkward gaps, inviting them to join in the prayers and hymns, and calling for some kind of response at the end. With reference to awkward gaps, how many times do people skip past a church service on their radio dial during the time the minister is collecting the offering plates and it appears to the listeners as if nothing is happening? If, on the other hand, the service is geared primarily to the radio audience, those in church feel as if they are observing a performance. The task is to make both the congregation and the radio audience part of the service.

Make the case. When speaking or preaching on the radio, the pastor as evangelist should always be an advocate for Jesus Christ. I believe the most winsome way to make the case is to confess your faith assumptions and show their reasonableness by sharing the confirming evidence of your own experience of God.

TELEVISION

The same principles apply to television as to radio, minus the rule of vocal compensation. When telecasting worship services, the worship leader's challenge is to maintain the sanctity of worship and not compromise theological integrity for the sake of popularity, nor capitulate to the manipulative techniques of the entertainment industry. Some televised religious programs come perilously close to doing that. The congregation becomes an audience; instead of worshipers they are observers of a performance designed for and geared to the viewing public.

Unlike the three mediums already discussed, television has the added dimension of visual identification, which imposes upon the television evangelist some additional rules for using this medium effectively.

Speak to persons. Talk to the camera as if you were talking to a person, because you *are* talking to people—you just can't see them. When you look into the camera with the red light, the viewer will be looking directly into your eyes. As in interpersonal witnessing, so too on television: Eye contact is crucial to effective communication. It's a matter of concentration.

Speak pleasantly. Try not to look like a sourpuss. To be pleasant is to look pleasant. We have good news, not bad news, for the world.

Speak with conviction. If you don't look as if you believe what you say, no one else is going to believe you either. You can speak with sincerity and conviction without being dogmatic or defensive.

Speak clearly. This is a matter not just of articulation and enunciation but also of vocabulary and sentence structure. Remember that the intellectual level of your television audience for the most part is not very high. Express your ideas as simply and clearly as possible. Don't get tangled up in complex sentences with too many relative clauses.

Speak interestingly. Whatever you do, be alert and lively. Make it interesting. To be dull is fatal. In church they may tune you out, but in their living room they can turn you off.

10

The Pastor's Contextual Considerations: Other Factors

The various elements that define the context for evangelism are not isolated from one another. Rather, they interrelate and intersect at many points. To simplify the discussion, I have grouped them here under three main headings: circumstances, receptivity, and cultural factors.

CIRCUMSTANCES

Of all factors this is the most difficult to isolate, because the possibilities for variation are infinite. Although a given evangelistic encounter may be similar in some or even many respects to another situation, it is nevertheless not feasible to try to categorize the possible circumstances, because every witnessing situation is unique, every human being is unique, every conversation is unique. The subject matter may be the same, but the persons could be different. The persons may be the same, but the time is different, for life has moved on and circumstances have changed since the last encounter. You can't step into the same evangelistic river twice.

It is possible, however, to identify some general groupings of circumstances that apply to every evangelistic encounter. Let me list four such classifications that affect the way one goes about the task of evangelism.

Locational circumstances. Where is the witnessing encounter taking place? In your study? Someone's living room? An open-air theater? On an airplane? Are you on your turf or their turf? Are you standing on a street corner? Sitting in a doctor's waiting room? Some locations are conducive to intimate conversation, some are not. Different settings call for different approaches. Open-air preaching, for example, makes its own demands of a speaker.[53] Lord Donald Soper has a brief but meaty chapter on that subject in a helpful little book edited by George Hunter, entitled *Rethinking Evangelism*. It is a stimulating introduction to an exciting form of evangelistic speaking, and it illustrates the impact of location.

Physical circumstances. These are related to locational circumstances, but I am thinking now specifically in terms of the physical facilities rather than the location. If, for example, you are in a living room, make sure the seating arrangement is advantageous and not detrimental to conversation. Avoid sitting so as to invite "sidetracking," "cross-firing," or "yoo-hooing"![54] Nor should you ever compete with a television set. If you are speaking in an auditorium or a large room, do you have the equipment and materials you need (blackboard, overhead projector, newsprint and easel, markers, tape recorder, slide projector, Bibles, writing materials, name tags, etc.)? Is there a public-address system, and does it work well? I would rather have no PA system than a poor one. It is a good idea to test the system before you speak, if that is convenient. How about the speaker's stand—is it the right height? Is the lighting satisfactory? What about the seating—is it comfortable? How is the room temperature—too hot or too cold? The answers to these kinds of questions may determine how long you speak, or how many breaks you take, or how heavy the content of your message should be.

Personal circumstances. With whom are you meeting? What is your relationship with them? Do you know them? Do they know you? Are there observers present? Why are they there? Why are you there: To entertain? Educate? Inform? Motivate? Do you have an "agenda"? Are you making an evangelistic call? A hospital call? A post-funeral call? Are you calling by yourself or with someone else? Are there special needs to be met? Are you speaking to a Rotary Club? Offering an invocation at the opening of the City Council? Preaching in a Reformed synagogue? Are the people to whom you are speaking Christians or non-Christians? Are they well-educated or illiterate? Rich or poor? Black or white? Male or female? Young or old? Business people or blue-collar workers? English-speaking or some other language? Once again, your approach will be influenced by your answers to these questions.

Programmatic circumstances. This category applies mainly to situations of a more formal nature, where the evangelistic speaker is part of a program of some sort. These are the kinds of programmatic circumstances that must be taken into consideration: What is the purpose of the occasion? What background information do you need and do you have about the event? Who is sponsoring it? What is the nature of the event: A funeral? A wedding? The dedication of a new building? A pregame ceremony? A Fourth of July celebration? A community fund drive? A civil rights demonstration? A men's breakfast? What is the schedule? Are you the only speaker? If there are others, what is the order of appearance and what are the different speakers doing? Is there a theme, or some plan for coordinating the topics? What are the other elements of the program? Is there any music? Where do you fit in? How will the program conclude? If you are the final speaker, what kind of close are they looking for: A climactic ending? An altar call? A rousing hymn? A prayer and benediction? If you are conducting a seminar or leading a workshop, how much time will you have, and how will the time be divided? Do you have the facilities you need to accommodate the format (such as breaking up into small discussion groups)?

The above categories are only a small sample of the circumstantial factors that define the context of evangelism. They should suffice to underscore the need for flexibility and to explain my personal aversion to canned approaches. Since every situation is unique, the pastor-evangelist must treat each situation as the circumstances demand. That calls for us to be good listeners, not overeager "soul winners" who can't wait to dump their own agenda on their quarry. Our witness must be related to the situation. We should have many arrows in our evangelism quivver, and we should know when, where, and how to use each arrow. No wonder Paul asked, "Who is sufficient for these things?" Thanks be to God, through Jesus Christ our Lord!

Only by the power of the Holy Spirit can we ever hope to do the work of an evangelist.

RECEPTIVITY

Remembering that the various factors being discussed are interconnected, let us look next at what may be called the receptivity factor. The related questions are intriguing: What is the nature of a faith decision? Is it rational, like a decision to take this or that job, to live here or there, or to buy this or that? Or is it more like a decision whether or not to marry someone? How does it differ in its givenness? That is, what is the difference between the gift of faith and inner assurance of another kind? Is it a dependent decision—does it depend on external factors beyond my control (a gift of God!) or internal factors that are nonrational (a precognitive disposition to believe)? Is it similar to other decisions in that I can be talked into it or out of it? Or in that I still have doubts about it once I've made it (something like the "buyers' remorse" that real estate agents talk about)? Or is the difference in the fact that I can't give the same kinds of reasons to validate my belief (i.e., my faith decision) as I can for a decision to purchase this or that? Or is the difference in the way a faith decision is confirmed or denied? How do I know when I've made the right decision?

One difference between a faith decision and other decisions would seem to be in the "proof" I summon to confirm it. I can make a rational case for other (non-faith) decisions, even if the choice is unclear. Non-faith decisions are arrived at deductively, whereas with faith decisions I *believe,* then I *prove* (faith seeking understanding). Faith "reasons" are after the fact.

What if my decision regarding a job, or a house, or my marriage is put into a faith context? That is to say, what if I am seeking the will of God in regard to that kind of decision? How does my faith approach affect how I decide? Is it by the way I interpret the results, the effects, and the impact of the decision? Does it have to do with the way I measure the rightness or wrongness of my choice? Or with my attitude about the decision and whatever happens as a result of it?

Again, what are the qualities in the *other* person (the hearer) that help or hinder a faith response to one's witness? Are there periods or moments of greater receptivity or resistance?[55] If there are, can they be identified? Classified? Anticipated? Predicted? Produced? How much does the hearer's response depend upon who the witness is? How much does it depend upon the style of the witness? Upon the personal qualities of the witness? Upon the hearer's sense of identity with the witness (similar interests, backgrounds, family circumstances, etc.)? Is it a matter of personality: attractiveness, charisma, persuasiveness, believability? What part does reputation play? The need for the other person's approval? Do some receivers (hearers) react more positively (or negatively) to certain senders than they do to others, or than others do to those same senders? If so, which ones? Why? Again, how significant is the timing? The setting? The style of the witness? The initial (opening) remarks? The content? Are there any principles that are universally applicable?

General Principles

My students and I have been wrestling with these and many such questions, and I am looking forward to sharing the results of our probe in a forthcoming book. For now there are some things that can be said with certainty concerning witnessing:

- It is helpful, if not necessary, to know where the hearer is and where she or he is coming from.

- The witness should try to plug into the hearer's life, enter the hearer's world, relate to and try to understand the hearer's experience.

- The witness, therefore, must herself or himself be a hearer first! That, of course, means being a good listener.

- That hearers respond in different ways to different witnesses at different times for different reasons is an observable reality. *Why* they do so is a mystery; *that* they do so is a fact.

So we can conclude that different people have to be evangelized in different ways, or appealed to in different ways. "Different strokes for different folks!" Or, to apply the same principle to the evangelization of people groups, different vibes for different tribes.

It is also safe to say that the hearer is less likely to be turned off, if

• The witness is perceived to be a genuinely caring person.

• The witness is not arrogant, insensitive, or rude.

• The witness does not put the hearer on the defensive by being judgmental or by appearing to be too high-and-mighty or holier-than-thou.

• The witness does not try to argue the hearer into the kingdom.

• The witness is, in short, a good listener!

In the dynamics of faith decision, the onus is not entirely on the witness. There are people who are not receptive to the gospel. If there is resistance, the sensitive witness will recognize it and try to understand it. What is the nature of the resistance? What is the extent of it? The reason for it? The intensity of it? The possibility of overcoming it? Is the resistant person an agnostic? An atheist? A disenchanted Christian? An adherent of another faith? What is his or her attitude: antagonism, apathy, arrogance? Is the reason stated the real reason, or is there a hidden agenda? Is the person's problem intellectual, emotional, spiritual, physical, financial, vocational, or volitional? Is it a matter of the heart, the mind, or the will? One can hardly be an effective witness without knowing such things about the other person. I shall have much more to say about this in the next chapter.

Reading and Responding to Receptivity

Receptivity is a matter of attitude. A person's attitude can change drastically, suddenly, and unexpectedly, for better or worse. The change can be viewed positively or negatively. Attitudes are both causative and symptomatic. Attitudes affect behavior. They cause people to act in certain ways. But attitudes themselves are caused by other factors and hence are symptomatic. The pastor-evangelist needs to know *why* a person feels the way she or he does. Why is that person resistant? The reason stated could be completely different from the real reason. The latter may be intentionally withheld or unintentionally buried deep in the person's subconscious. The surface reason may be quite plausible and even apparent.

Hidden meanings are usually more determinative of attitudes than surface reasons. "I'm furious at the church for taking my grandson off the roll!" That's a surface reason and is certainly a causative factor. But is there any hidden reason for the grandmother's anger? Maybe she is angry not just because they took her grandson off the roll but because she had a bad experience as a child in Sunday school, or maybe she can't reconcile her own relationship to the church with her being an alcoholic, or maybe she is having serious doubts about her faith, or maybe she is behind in her financial commitment to the church and her anger is a way of justifying her not paying it. Is there a hidden source of her hostility? Too often in our interpersonal witnessing we respond to surface reasons instead of the real causes of defection, probably because we don't listen carefully enough, or we don't ask the right questions, or we overreact to what people tell us. So the stewardship callers report that the Jacksons are "mad at the church" because of the denomination's stand on South African investments. Is that any reason for the Jacksons to stop worshiping God?

The pastor-evangelist must read carefully the signs of receptivity or resistance and respond appropriately. The receptivity of the hearer determines the pace of the witness. The lower the receptivity the slower the pace. The slower the pace the more listening is needed. Don't rush it, and don't force it. Never impose your witness upon someone else. Go slow with those who are resistant. Back off and listen. On the other hand, be ready to respond to the receptive person, striking while the iron is hot, so to speak. If a person wants to share, by all means share!

My inclination—indeed, my desire—is to fly with those who want to fly, run with those who want to run, and walk with those who are ready only to walk. If you're running and they're walking, you will be too far ahead and soon out of sight. Fly with the fliers, run with the runners, and walk with the walkers.

The task is to encourage the walkers to run, the runners to fly, and those who are standing still to start walking. It is also to encourage the sitters to stand! All this is done better by pulling than by pushing, but not in a condescending or patronizing way. Do not lose touch with where the unreceptive person is, for you yourself may have been there too. But you cannot help someone to come to Christ if you yourself are not with Christ.

Once again, all this points up the need for would-be witnesses to be good listeners and for would-be listeners to depend on the Holy Spirit, who alone can give us the sensitivity to listen wisely, to relate compassionately, and to respond unselfishly.

CULTURAL FACTORS

There are countless cultural factors that also bear upon the work of the evangelist. Some of the more important ones to be considered follow.

The Race Factor

The question is simply this: Can the love of Jesus Christ transcend racial barriers that reflect the sinfulness of humanity and the evils of society? The pastor-evangelist must believe that it can. My own experience in multiracial churches whose members discovered and celebrated their oneness in Christ is a testimony to the truth that it does! That experience and others are the reason for my resistance to the homogeneous unit principle. In a society where racial bigotry and prejudice persist, where class consciousness is greater than we care to admit, and where economic discrimination and political injustice are everyday realities for far too many minority people, we do not serve well the cause of human freedom or of Christ by encouraging a separatist mentality that contradicts our affirmations of Christian unity.

The fact that many people do not want to cross racial lines to join a church is, I say, a manifestation of human sin. To translate it into an evangelistic principle that tempts Christians to seek first "people like us" provides a convenient excuse for too many churches to ignore the call to an inclusive outreach. The danger is that success, instead of faithfulness, becomes the measure of our ministry, and the integrity of evangelism is compromised by the expediency of a convenient rationale.

To be sure, the pastor-evangelist must be aware of and come to grips with the race barrier. As a white pastor seeking to relate to the black people who were moving into our community, I discovered several principles.

People want to believe in people. Our black neighbors wanted to believe that they really would be welcome in what was then a white church. They wanted to believe in us, but we had to win our right to be heard and prove our sincerity. After all, they had plenty of reason to distrust any white people, after centuries of slavery and continued discrimination.

Outreach is the key. What convinced the blacks they were welcome was the fact that we didn't sit back and wait for them to come. We reached out to them.

Persistence is the proof. The proof of our sincerity was the fact that we kept reaching out, even if the initial reception was negative. Our callers would not take no for an answer but kept coming back again and again, as long as the person or persons had no church affiliation. It was slow going at first. But the blacks gradually began to come, as our persistence prevailed, and soon blacks and whites were calling together on black and white neighbors. We were becoming a genuinely integrated congregation.

Assimilation is crucial. That is true for anyone who joins a church, but it is especially true for those who cross racial lines to do it. Preparation for membership was a significant experience for our new black members, who relished the opportunity to learn about the history and beliefs of their new church and who took seriously their membership vows. Some had had no previous church background, and some were coming from a totally different worship tradition, but they made the transition eagerly and easily. Assimilation is a process that should lead to involvement in all aspects of the life of the church.

Inclusiveness is the way. We were becoming an inclusive congregation, discovering the excitement of unity in diversity. Our new members were making the transition easily because we were not asking them to become "like us." We had our traditional ways of doing things, but there were changes, too, as our congregational life reflected the contributions of blacks and whites alike and of all the cultures represented in the membership.

I believe these principles would hold true for the black church that would like to reach out to whites. Unfortunately, not many of them do. It is not that whites are not welcome in black churches. On the contrary, whites will find a warmer welcome in a black church than in most white churches. But very few black churches have sought to evangelize whites. That's too bad, because I think there are whites who would respond to a persistent evangelistic outreach from a caring black congregation. It is not easy, but it can be done. This conviction leads me to urge every pastor not to hesitate to evangelize across racial lines. The Holy Spirit can and does change human hearts, and those whom the Spirit touches will respond to a man or woman of God, regardless of race. The love of Christ constrains us to be color-blind evangelists.

The Language Factor

Interpersonal witnessing presupposes two-way communication, and communication presupposes a common language. In order for the gospel to be heard, it must be expressed in language that is understood by the receiver. It is incumbent upon the evangelist, therefore, to know the language of those to whom the gospel is proclaimed. The best rule is, If you don't know the language of the people to whom you are ministering, learn it! There are other things to be said about this, however.

What if you don't speak the language? If you are an itinerant evangelist, preaching in different countries whose languages you do not have time to learn, or if you are making a one-time presentation to a group whose language you do not know, you should use an interpreter. It should be someone who can convey your same spirit and fervor and your same emphasis. Adjust your pace accordingly and try to establish a rhythm between the two of you that captures the feeling of your words.

When do actions speak louder than words? The greater the language barrier, the more important nonverbal communication becomes. People resort to their own makeshift sign languages when they try to communicate with someone whose language they cannot speak. You do not have to speak the other person's language to communicate basic human emotions. People can tell by looking at your face whether you are hostile or friendly. Gestures, touching, and facial expressions, with a smattering of word sounds, communicate more than we sometimes realize.

When is a language barrier a barrier? Language can be a barrier even when both speak the same language. The problem is not only the words we use but how we pronounce them and how we use them. Words can mean different things to different people, as New Yorkers who visit London and Londoners who visit New York quickly learn! The problem is compounded by dialect and accent, not to mention grammar and syntax, all of which suggest that overcoming a language barrier involves more than merely learning to speak the textbook version.

When is a barrier not a barrier? The love of Christ can transcend even the language barrier. That's the other side of the coin. People who may not understand your words can sense your Christian love. Explanations rely upon words, but love can be experienced without being explained. Some of the people who responded to our evangelistic calling in Philadelphia spoke little or no English, but they attended our membership preparation classes and joined the church, because of the Christian fellowship they experienced in a caring congregation. Sometimes family members or friends would serve as interpreters for them, but often they would come alone, relying on what little English they could understand. In the meantime, the church offered English classes for our Spanish-speaking members and Spanish classes for our English-speaking members. As their verbal skills improved, those for whom English was not their native tongue were then able to respond to the teaching and preaching ministries of the church. But what brought them initially was not a verbal but a visible gospel, revealed in the lives of those who reached out to them in Christian love.

The Religious Factor

It matters greatly whether or not the person with whom you wish to share your faith is a Christian, an adherent of another faith, or a nonbeliever. If the other person's religion is different, how should a pastor-evangelist share her or his faith? Here are a few suggestions regarding interfaith dialogue.

Share the why of faith. Plug into the other person's God-consciousness. Instead of asking questions that make people feel the need to defend or explain their beliefs, invite them to share their experience of God. Talk about the *why* of faith. Help them to recognize and articulate their faith assumptions and to acknowledge the givenness of faith. Listen for plug-in points, where your experience can relate to theirs.

Affirm the positive. Call attention to the points of agreement and similarity in your perceptions of God and of your experiences of the presence of God. Talk about prayer and the disciplines of the spiritual life. Share your aspirations for peace on earth and good will among all peoples.

Be open to truth. God can speak to us through persons of other faiths. Many of the doctrines of Christianity have their parallels in other religions. Those who engage in interfaith dialogue should never be dogmatic, judgmental, or argumentative. Such an attitude precludes the possibility of a faith-sharing conversation. Be open and responsive to what is true and reasonable and good.

Make your witness! To be open to the faith of others does not mean to compromise one's own faith. On the contrary, true dialogue implies that those involved have a point of view that deserves to be heard. We Christians have something to say about the universal quest for truth, and we can say it with conviction and power, once we have won the right to be heard. An intolerant spirit will not gain us that right. We need to remember that the truth of Christianity is Jesus Christ. The question is how best to bear witness to him?

When sharing faith with adherents of other religions, I have found the best way to proceed is to ask them how they feel about Jesus Christ. Draw them out regarding their beliefs about Jesus and then gently and tactfully dispel any misconceptions they may have. This is a time to share the *what* of faith, all the while checking to see if your words are being understood. Move from there back to the *why* of your faith, acknowledging that your faith is a gift and that you can't prove it any more than they can prove theirs. Then you can share the confirming evidence of your faith assumption and invite them to do likewise. Now you are talking on the same level, and the result should be a beautiful experience of faith sharing.

11
The Pastor's Evangelistic Style

Before presuming to define an evangelistic style, I must stress a basic principle of this entire book: It is God who converts human hearts. If I may paraphrase the psalmist, unless the Lord builds the evangelistic house, the evangelist will labor in vain. Without the Holy Spirit, all our marketing methods, packaged programs, and reasonable rules are full of sound and fury, signifying nothing. One can easily lose sight of that truth in an effort to understand our human role as God's instruments in the evangelistic enterprise. We do have a responsibility, and that is what we are trying to define and understand, especially that of the pastor who takes seriously Paul's admonition to do the work of an evangelist.

It is in that spirit, then, that I want to address the difficult question of style, for I am convinced that doing the work of an evangelist has more to do with style than with method. Indeed, I am not offering or advocating a particular program. Rather, I have for years been appealing for an evangelism that has theological integrity, based on an epistemological approach to faith and a theology of the church that takes seriously our ministry as the servant people of God.

Such an evangelism calls for a particular style that is quite different from the sometimes overly aggressive approaches employed by some well-intentioned churches. I have called it "service evangelism," which expression is intended to suggest not that service is evangelism but that service and evangelism are concomitant aspects of ministry. I considered calling it "servant evangelism," but that connoted something slightly different, placing the emphasis more on the service *of* evangelism. I wanted to convey the idea not of a servant doing evangelism (although that is certainly a valid concept) but of an evangelism that is service-oriented, the purpose of which is not just saving souls but saving lives and helping people. So we are talking about a style, not a method. It is not *the* style but *a* style, one that is more incarnational than propositional, more dialogic than dogmatic, more relational than proclamational. A method is fixed and rigid; a style can blend consistency with flexibility.

QUALITIES OF AN EFFECTIVE WITNESS

Realizing that interpersonal evangelism does entail the oral communication of the gospel, and assuming a pastor wants to be an effective witness for Christ, what are the desirable human qualities? As I have already stressed (see Chapter 4), one must first have one's own faith house in order. That being the case, here are some guidelines for an effective witness.

Be friendly, not hostile. Friendliness is the first and most obvious trait to be desired. Friendly people make friends; hostile people make enemies. Friendly people are approachable; hostile people are intimidating. A hostile witness is as unhelpful in the living room as in the courtroom. Misanthropy and evangelism are mutually exclusive. A pastor-evangelist has to be someone who really likes people—a people person!

Be caring, not callous. The other person has to feel as if he or she is talking to someone who cares, someone who listens empathically. People don't want to share their joys or their sorrows with a callous person. The style of the witness must represent and convey the compassion and availability of a caring community, whose mission is one of justice, peace, and love and whose calling is to minister to human needs in the name of Christ. By its faithfulness to that mission and calling, the church wins the right to be heard.

Be affirming, not condemning. You are not likely to win friends and influence people by condemning them. An effective witness affirms other people, and when you do that they respond affirmatively.

Be direct, not devious. An effective witness does not beat around the bush but is forthright and direct. One can be direct without being abrasive, forthright without being brutally frank. The other person should not have to be puzzled by confusing implications and confounded by devious statements and subtle innuendos.

Be honest, not hypocritical. Honesty is indispensable to the integrity of evangelism. Don't say things you don't mean or claim things that are not true. To do so is hypocritical, and the unmasking of hypocrisy is devastating to one's credibility.

Be sincere, not synthetic. Say what you mean and mean what you say. Don't pretend to feel something you don't feel. Your sympathetic response to what you hear should be genuine, not something you turn on for effect. People will eventually see through a synthetic concern.

Be enthusiastic, not depressed. Enthusiasm is contagious. An enthusiastic faith is a contagious faith. To be enthusiastic you have to act enthusiastically. If you are not enthusiastic about Jesus Christ, you can hardly excite anyone else about him. To be depressed is to be depressing.

Be open-minded, not closed-minded. The witness must also be open-minded: approachable, reasonable, willing to consider a new idea or a different approach. A closed-minded, stubborn person does not stimulate faith sharing. Openness is a highly commendable quality in any witness for Christ.

Be personal, not private. To be effective, a witness must be willing to share and to relate in a personal way. Faith sharing is a two-way street. It is harder to get close to a private person. People who are willing to share themselves make it easier for others to do the same.

Be vulnerable, not defensive. There is a risk in being personal, however. You can be hurt by someone who misunderstands, misconstrues, or misuses what you have shared about yourself. A Christian witness is willing to accept that risk and to be vulnerable. It entails leading from weakness rather than from strength; that is, acknowledging one's faith struggles rather than presenting oneself as a paragon of virtue and a tower of spiritual strength. To be defensive is to shift the focus of our witness from our Savior to ourselves.

Interpersonal dialogue calls for the witness to be listening, not lecturing the other person; to be building bridges, not barriers to understanding; to be seeking to clarify, not to cloud the issues. Effective witnesses are always looking for points of contact rather than points of contradiction, things with which they can agree rather than things with which they disagree, what's right about what the other person says rather than what's wrong with it.

There are people who insist on taking a contrary view to everything that is said. Instead of acknowledging the general rule, they would rather argue about the exception. They believe nothing should be unanimous. They pour sand into the gears of progress. I call them "but" people. They're always saying, "Yes, but. . . . " But this, but that, but everything. Lord, deliver us from "but" people!

SUITING THE APPROACH TO THE PERSON

In one-to-one evangelism, the witness should first try to discern where the other person is coming from, in order to suit the approach to the person. Experience with all kinds of people should enable pastors to read people very well. The following basic dividing points will determine the approach to be used.

Member or not a member of your church. Let's assume the person's name is Tillie Tollhouse. The first dividing point is whether or not she is a member of your church. It makes a world of difference in the way you relate to her. Your assumptions and your agenda with inactive members are different from what they are with nonmembers. Those who are on the rolls, even if they are backsliding, have a claim on the church and may feel much closer to it than their church activity indicates. I was often surprised at the friendliness of some people I seldom saw in church. When I would encounter them at some social gathering, they would introduce me warmly to their companions and speak with great enthusiasm about the church. They would have been horrified and terribly hurt were I to have acted as if they were anything but the most loyal members of the congregation. The pastor-evangelist can build on that relationship. If they are apathetic or bored, to use John Savage's epithets,[56] your hope is that your witness will be the channel through which the Holy Spirit may win them back. If Tillie is not a member of your church, there is another major dividing point.

Member of another church or unchurched. If you discover she is a member of another church, you would try to find out whether or not she is active. If she is, fine; if not, encourage her to become active in her present church. If she is looking for a church of a different denomination from yours, refer her to the nearest church of that denomination; someone from your church should check back a few weeks later, however, to see if she has heard from the other church. If, on the other hand, Tillie is completely unchurched, then you need to know something else about her, before you know what your approach should be.

Believer in God or nonbeliever. Does she believe in God? In Christ? Relate to her on that level, inviting her to share her faith experience and asking sensitive questions about her relationship to or feelings about Christ. If she believes in Christ, you would want to find out her church background and, by asking more questions, help her to see the incongruity between loving Christ and neglecting the church which he loved and of which he is Lord. If Tillie says she does not believe in God or Christ, the next thing you need to know is whether or not she is what I call a "seeker after truth." This is the crucial evangelistic question and the basic dividing point.

A seeker or not a seeker. If Tillie is a genuine seeker, she is winnable. David's word to Solomon is true for us as well: "If you seek him, he will be found by you" (1 Chron. 28:9). Jesus' words are good news to a seeker: "Ask, and it will be given you; seek, and you will find; knock, and it will be opened to you" (Luke 11:9). Seekers are more than halfway there. The Holy Spirit is already at work, prompting them in their quest for truth. It is not difficult to discover if someone is a seeker after truth. If she appears not to be, there is something else that will affect the way you proceed with her.

Reasonable or unreasonable. If Tillie is a reasonable person, someone who speaks reasonably and is willing to listen to reason, you can have a meaningful and productive conversation with her, in the course of which she may well respond to a reasonable presentation of the gospel. As a reasonable person, she would have to agree that the gospel promises are indeed good news. That does not mean she would be ready to make a commitment to Jesus Christ, but it would be a step in the right direction. She would have to ask herself if a reasonable person can refuse to be a seeker after truth. If Tillie is an unreasonable person, there is yet another distinction that will determine your approach to her.

Friendly or unfriendly. People can be unreasonable without being unfriendly. I have known some like that. If Tillie turns out to be that kind of person, you can linger a little longer in hopes that some point of contact will surface in the conversation. Since she will not listen to reason, there is no reason to reason! But if she is friendly, she may let you share your faith, and she may appreciate your availability. Chances are, however, that she will be unfriendly as well as unreasonable. If that's the case, don't waste her time or yours. "Shake off the dust!" (Matt. 10:14).

Those words of Jesus are a proof text for getting out, not for giving up! Offer your friendship and, if it seems appropriate, your availability in the future; then leave. But don't give up on her. Give Tillie's name to the intercessory prayer circle and have someone call on her again in a few months. Who knows? Maybe she will have had a change of mind and heart. The Holy Spirit can work miracles for the likes of Tillie!

The distinctions I have described are graphically displayed in the diagram. I have not attempted to discuss all the possibilities represented in the chart and the ramifications thereof. One glance is sufficient to show how much there is to know about someone in order to fit the approach to the person, and how utterly inappropriate it is to use the same set spiel for everyone. What is called for is a relational style and a listening stance.

THE ART OF LISTENING

The clue to effective interpersonal witnessing is the art of listening. I view as a promising development the proliferation of workshops and seminars devoted to helping people develop

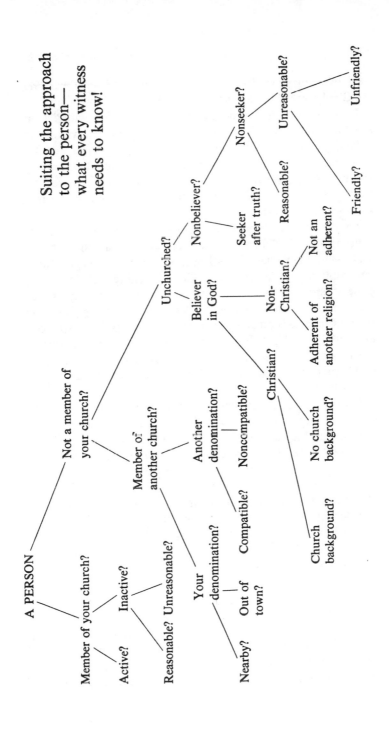

Suiting the approach to the person—what every witness needs to know!

their listening skills. For mnemonic purposes I have proffered six C rules for listening, which are repeated below in brief.[57]

Compassion. The word means literally "suffer with," from the Latin *com* (with) and *patio* (suffer). The motivation for listening is the compassion of the listener. It is to *be with* the other person. It is the touchstone of incarnational witnessing, and the mark of a caring heart. If you really care, you feel the hurt and share the pain of the other person, and that person knows you have listened.

Concentration. Good listening requires concentration, and concentration is difficult when there are distracting sights or sounds. Interpersonal witnessing should be as free as possible of interruptions and disturbances. Good listening includes paying close attention to facial expressions and body language, which often speak much louder than words. Recognizing that your thought process is much faster than the other person's speaking rate, you should use the time differential to reflect on what is being said and to search for meaning, rather than letting your mind wander off somewhere. The discipline will enhance your concentration.

Control. What I mean by control is knowing when to speak and when not to speak. Good listeners are not threatened by silence, and they are able to suspend judgment and avoid rash assumptions or premature conclusions. They know when and how to wait before responding. Some people feel they have to fill every conversational gap with words. Good listeners can resist that temptation. They control their impulsive utterances and do not interrupt the other person.

Comprehension. Listening implies comprehension. When the speaker's words go in one ear and out the other, this proves there is nothing between the ears to stop them! Good listeners are always seeking to comprehend what the other person is saying and to understand the implications of the spoken words. They know the difference between what is happening and what is going on. Comprehension is the best antidote to anger. You are less likely to be angry with someone if you know *why* that person feels the way he or she does. To discover the *why* you must listen through the words to the deeper meaning. Plug into what Urban Holmes termed "the deep memory."[58]

Clarification. Comprehension depends on clarification. A good listener makes sure that what is heard is what is said and that what is said is what is meant. This assurance, in turn, requires feedback, in which process the listener restates to the speaker what the listener has heard. That gives the speaker a chance to confirm, correct, modify, or amplify what he or she first said. Then the listener rephrases in the listener's own words the impact and meaning of what was said, to the speaker's satisfaction. "Is this what you mean, Bill—that the church ought not to take stands on *any* controversial issues?" The purpose of feedback is clarification: to see if the other person feels you understand.

Commitment. The listener is not a sphinx. Good listening is an active activity, not a passive one. It includes being ready, willing, and able to respond appropriately to what is being said. By appropriately I mean not only verbally but in whatever other ways the situation demands or suggests. A relationship has been established, and if the listener doesn't respond to the outpouring of the other person's soul, then that person can hardly feel she or he has been heard. Good listening implies a commitment on the part of the Christian witness to be available and to follow through.

I cannot emphasize strongly enough the importance of listening in interpersonal communication. One must listen to understand, and one should understand before responding. Just as it is prudent to look before you leap, so it is wise to listen before you "peep"! As a Christian witness, your listening is not an end in itself. Active listening, we said, must issue in a response.

THE FOUR POINTS OF FAITH SHARING

The next question, then, is what sort of response? Because every individual is unique, we cannot have one all-purpose response, no matter to whom or to what we are responding. But since we are talking about a style and not a method, I should like to offer some principles that are applicable to any situation. They are intended to guide and not to restrict the witness, to suggest how to respond, not what to say. I call them the four points of faith sharing.

The faith-sharing approach to interpersonal witnessing and evangelism is defined and described in Chapter 2. The question is, How does the witness facilitate or bring about a faith-sharing conversation? What can the pastor-evangelist or anyone else say to the other person that will "open the door of faith"?[39] My proposed answer to this need is for the witness to be aware of four points of contact with the other person, which are distinct but related. The word *point* has a double meaning, referring both to a conversational moment calling for a particular response on the part of the witness and to the idea, statement, or action on the part of the other person which precipitates that moment.

Come-in points. The witness should be listening for opportunities to ask a faith question. As the other person relates a meaningful experience, be it happy, sad, challenging, or whatever, the witness might say, "What part has your faith played in all this?" or, "What has this experience meant to your faith?" This kind of question does not put the other person on the defensive but, rather, allows that person to reply at whatever level he or she wants. It is a surprisingly disarming approach, simple and easy. And it is amazing how readily people respond. They almost inevitably do, and when they do, the conversation is instantly transformed into a faith-sharing experience, whether their response is a testimony of faith or a shared feeling of doubt, anger, or guilt. Either one is a faith response. Come-in points are invitational; you invite and listen.

Plug-in points. The meaning of this expression should be clear from its frequent use throughout this book. Plug-in points are the switchboard for the faith-sharing exchange, the sockets where your faith can plug into the other person's faith experience. In interpersonal witnessing, this is the point you are always hoping to attain. The task here is relational. You affirm and relate to the other person's faith experience, being careful not to overpower or overshadow the person you are hoping to reach. The goal is to encourage that person to share his or her faith. There will be an opportunity for you to tell your story, but first you must be a listener. "That's a beautiful story, Jean. Isn't it wonderful how things seem to work out, when you put your trust in God? I had a similar experience just the other day...." Or it may be a faith struggle that you have in common. Whatever the plug-in point, you can build on the relationship you have established and, by sensitive questioning, bring the conversation around to Christ. "You say you don't belong to a church, Pat, but you certainly have a strong faith in God. How do you feel about Jesus Christ?"

Take-on points. There are times when you may have to challenge a faith contradiction. You would want to do this in a positive and constructive way, of course, not by assaulting other people but by asking questions that help them to see the reasonableness of a contrary point of view or the logical inconsistency of their own. Whereas come-in points are invitational and plug-in points are relational, take-on points are confrontational, but you confront by appealing to reason rather than resorting to attack. "You say nobody ever calls on you from the church, nobody cares. Well, *we're* here. Would we be here if we didn't care?" There are two important rules to keep in mind with respect to take-on points.

Rule One: Be up front with your feelings. If you are worrying about how to broach the subject or whether to make your witness, say so. For example, suppose you were calling on an inactive member and, after a very friendly visit, you were worried lest you destroy the effect of your call by bringing up the subject. You might say something like this: "You know, Mr. Brown, I've enjoyed this visit so much that I'm afraid I've stayed longer than I should. And I'm embarrassed that I never got around to mentioning my main reason for being here. Will I jeopardize the relationship we've established here tonight if I bring it up now?" If your intentions are worthy and your concern is sincere, you can and should be open in expressing your feelings.

Rule Two: You can say the hard thing if your face language and body language communicate an accepting spirit and a caring heart. "I understand you are very upset about that, John, but is it really any reason for not worshiping God?" Or, "Tell me,

Bill, do you feel that people should stop coming to church whenever something happens with which they disagree?" Or, "I really care about you, Mary, and it's because I do that I feel I have to say (whatever it is)."

Take-off points. It is sometimes necessary to answer a faith question or to clarify a faith confusion. Take-off points are informational. The objective of the witness is to inform or to explain. So when Maggie says, "I'm embarrassed to say I don't know what the word *gospel* means," this is not the time to psychoanalyze her ("Does it really bother you that you don't know that word?"). If Maggie wants to know what the word means, for goodness' sake tell her! But you don't have to give her the whole load at once; answer her question and then pause to see what else is on her mind. The object is not to belabor the take-off point but to find another plug-in point. The witness should not be trapped into becoming a question answerer, for the questions may be the asker's way of avoiding Jesus' question, "Who do you say that I am?" It is important to inform, explain, and clarify, but such conversation is head-to-head, not heart-to-heart, talk. To get back on the faith-sharing level, you could say something like this: "I'd like to ask you a question, Maggie. Now that you know what all these words mean, what difference does it make in terms of your relationship with Jesus Christ?"

The Socratic Approach

There is another rule pertaining to this style of interpersonal witnessing: It is better to ask questions than to give answers. Answers deny the other person the joy of discovery. Contradictory statements tend to force the other person into a defensive position; they evoke the need to defend a point of view. Sensitive questioning, on the other hand, can help people to verbalize those assumptions and to discover whether or not their conclusions are consistent with their assumptions. You will know that you have been asking the right questions when someone says, "I see what you mean," and you have never said what you mean! The other person has simply recognized the logical conclusion implied in the answer to the question you asked. What is recommended, therefore, is a Socratic approach to witnessing: asking questions that help the other person to discover the answers for himself or herself.

Summary

As should be apparent from what has been said about them, the four points of faith sharing are by no means mutually exclusive. In the dynamics of interpersonal witnessing, the conversation can bounce from point to point. There is a time to affirm and a time to inform, a time to invite and a time to relate, a time to explain and a time to confront, a time to speak and a time to listen. The four points of faith sharing can be summarized succinctly as follows:

Come-in points	**Take-on points**
Invitational	Confrontational
Ask a faith question	Challenge a faith contradiction
Invite; listen	Point out; reason

Plug-in points	**Take-off points**
Relational	Informational
Share a faith experience	Clarify a faith confusion
Affirm; relate	Explain; inform

In this chapter I have attempted to define not a method but a style of interpersonal witnessing by considering the qualities desired in an effective witness, the importance of suiting the approach to the person, some guidelines for listening, and some ways to encourage or facilitate faith sharing.[60] The assumption underlying all these ideas and suggestions is that the interpersonal witnessing we are describing will take place in the context of the mission of the church as the servant people of God.

12

The Pastor's Spiritual Rewards

To be a faithful and effective pastor-evangelist is a tremendous challenge. It takes a degree of ability, a level of commitment, and a combination of qualities that no pastor with a speck of modesty would claim to possess. But to accept the challenge has its rewards, even for those of us who feel unequal and inadequate to the task.

Personal Growth

One thing is sure: The pastor who strives to do the work of an evangelist will grow in the effort—spiritually, theologically, and emotionally.

Spiritual growth. I have pointed out more than once that to be an effective evangelist one has to have one's own faith house in order. This does not mean, of course, that one is sure of all the answers. It means understanding one's own faith. One has to know *why* one believes before one can make a case for believing. As a pastor-evangelist you will grow spiritually because you will realize more than anyone else that you cannot do the work of an evangelist without God. The Holy Spirit is the Converter of human hearts. You and I are only the instruments through whom the Spirit works to change people's lives. The Spirit convicts them of their sin, convinces them of their need of a Savior, and converts them to Jesus Christ. Knowing that, you and I had best enter into this ministry on our knees. We cannot do that without growing spiritually.

Theological growth. As an evangelist you will grow theologically, for you have to know what you believe before you can talk to someone else about God. When you think evangelistically, you grow theologically. The practice of apologetics will make you more articulate as a preacher, as a teacher, and as a witness to and advocate of Jesus Christ. Would that more theologians were evangelists! I have come to see that theology has difficulty speaking to the world. Theology is the church's conversation with itself; evangelism is the church's conversation with the world. An effective evangelist can transmit theological concepts and spiritual truths to the world in terms that the world can understand. That is something theologians must learn to do. It is the evangelist who has maintained and must maintain the dialogue with the secular disciplines, and to do that the evangelist must be theologically competent as well as capable of communicating the gospel. The more one engages in dialogue with the world, the more aware one becomes of the world's way of thinking; the more aware one is, the better able one is to relate the gospel to the world's needs. The pastor-evangelist, therefore, cannot help growing theologically.

Emotional growth. When you do the work of an evangelist you also grow emotionally, for you have a greater sense of power, of direction, and of joy. You will be aware of a new power in your preaching, teaching, counseling, and all the other areas of ministry, because you have a sense of God's presence and involvement in your life and work. The power is God's power, of course, but because you believe in a personal God whose grace is sufficient and whose power is made perfect in human weakness, you go about your ministry with greater confidence.

Doing the work of an evangelist also gives you a new sense of direction. It helps you to keep your priorities in order. You know why you are there and where you are heading. You feel a sense of the urgency and importance of what you are doing, a new awareness of your call to ministry, and a deeper appreciation of what it means to be a servant of and witness to Jesus Christ.

At the same time you will discover a new joy in being a pastor. Where does the joy come from? Is it from the "warm fuzzies" you receive at the door of the church after one of your sterling sermons? Is it from the experience of being surrounded by a loving, caring, affirming, appreciative group of parishioners, your own little flock, who need you and look to you for leadership and guidance and encouragement and comfort? Of course you derive joy from all these things, including the warm fuzzies. But there is no greater joy than helping *another* person to discover the joy of knowing, loving, and serving Jesus Christ. Every step forward in faith that you help someone else take is a reason for joy.

It is not that you can take credit for what happens but that you can rejoice in the knowledge that God has used you to work his miracles of grace. You do not always know when and if that has happened or is happening, or even whether it will happen. But every now and then God allows you the unmatchable privilege of knowing that it *has* happened and that you were part of it. When a member of your flock comes up to you some day and says, "Thank you, Pastor, you have helped me discover what it really means to trust God," you know something of the joy John felt when he wrote in his third letter, "No greater joy can I have than this, to hear that my children follow the truth" (v. 4). God has a way of giving us just enough of these satisfying moments to keep us going—just enough. To keep us from becoming too elated by the abundance of revelations, he also gives us a few thorns in the flesh to harass us and keep us humble! For the pastor-evangelist, the joy of being used by God to lead an unbeliever or someone who was not a Christian into a relationship with Christ and the church is at least as great as the joy of seeing believers grow in their faith.

The Impact on Others

Along with the personal growth that your evangelistic work makes possible, there is also the reality of the impact of your ministry on others. As a pastor-evangelist, you can take much satisfaction from the fact that the results of your work will be multiplying not just arithmetically but geometrically. Evangelism has a duplicating effect. Every person whose life is touched by your ministry begins a chain reaction you could not stop if you wanted to. The person you touch influences someone else, who in turn touches someone else, who may have two children, one of whom goes to seminary and becomes a pastor and touches hundreds of other lives, who in turn touch thousands, and on and on it goes. How exciting it is when you hear about your first spiritual grandchild, someone who was led to Christ by someone you have led to Christ! It staggers the mind to think how many grandchildren, and great-grandchildren, and great-great-great-great-great-grandchildren in the faith every pastor-evangelist will have. Do you think you can't make a difference? Can you possibly believe you don't make a difference?

There is no way you could begin to measure the impact of your evangelistic ministry, but that it can and will be part of a chain of faith involving hundreds, even thousands of people, about whom you will never know or hear, is a spiritual fact of life. It is not the immediate and visible results that measure the impact of your influence, for the chain reaction is as limitless as the future itself. As long as day follows night, the ripples from your splash in the pond of faith will continue to fan out into people's lives. You and I are here today, in ministry, because of the influence of many, many persons on other persons years ago. What a thrilling thought!

Of course, you are not the only one who will have an influence on the thousands of persons in your chain of faith. Many other persons will have touched their lives along the way to Christ. But you will have played your part in their pilgrimages. The times you are privileged to hear about your involvement in someone else's faith story are probably more the exception than the rule. But for the pastor-evangelist they happen often enough to sustain you in those low periods, when you wonder what in the world you have accomplished and whether anybody is really listening to anything you have to say. That is when another spiritual carrot helps to keep you going, another one of God's reminders that you have assisted people in their faith journey, and that God has used you to help them to know the Christ whom you know, and to love and obey him as their Savior and Lord.

The Impact on the Church

While the pastor can be and too often is the bottleneck to evangelism, the pastor as evangelist can also be a catalyst for growth. When you do the work of an evangelist, your church will grow—numerically as well as spiritually. That is a source of immense satisfaction to any pastor. While statistical growth is not the measure of one's faithfulness, it is certainly something to be celebrated joyfully and gratefully when it occurs. It is much more likely to occur if the evangelistic burden does not rest upon the shoulders of the pastor alone but is accepted as the responsibility of the entire congregation. Not every church member can do the work of an evangelist, but there is something everyone can do to contribute to the church's evangelistic ministry. The pastor as evangelist must lead the way, for doing the work of an evangelist also includes training others for the task. The satisfaction of having equipped the church to be the evangelist is an even greater blessing to a pastor than his or her personal evangelism.

But for the church to be the evangelist,[61] the *pastor* must be an evangelist. When the pastor is excited and enthusiastic about his or her faith, the members of the congregation are much more likely to be excited and enthusiastic about their faith. And when they are, the church will grow spiritually and probably numerically, because enthusiastic faith is contagious.

Church growth is both a goal and a by-product of evangelism, but not the reason for it. The reason for evangelism is the mandate laid upon us by Jesus, the church, and the world. Faithfulness to Jesus Christ is not measured by worldly success. On the contrary, the way of our Lord is the way of the cross. That is why our ultimate satisfaction is not to be tied to church budgets and membership rolls. Our greatest spiritual reward is the satisfaction of knowing that we are striving to do God's will.

So as you do the work of an evangelist, let the apostle Paul's charge to the Corinthians be my charge to you: "Be steadfast, immovable, always abounding in the work of the Lord, knowing that in the Lord your labor is not in vain."

Appendix A

Sample of Pastors' Concerns About Evangelism

Category	Number	Percent
The Meaning of Evangelism	*162*	*30.9*

Looking for a viable style of evangelism (42)

Concerned about the theology of evangelism (38)

Problems with evangelism in a pluralistic society (31)

What is the proper definition of evangelism? (31)

What is the relation between mission and evangelism? (5)

Concerned about radio and TV evangelism (5)

What is the relation between stewardship and evangelism? (3)

What is the relation between evangelism and church growth? (3)

What is *the* gospel? (2)

How to be evangelistic and ecumenical at the same time (1)

How does evangelism relate to faith healing? (1)

Attitudinal Problems	*85*	*16.2*

How to communicate my own faith (14)

How to share my faith with integrity (13)

Category	Number	Percent

"I'm not motivated enough to motivate others." (10)

What is the pastor's role in evangelism? (10)

Need to deal with my own fears re evangelism (10)

Need to increase my own spirituality (8)

Lack of commitment to evangelism (8)

Need to deal with my own negative attitude (5)

How to deal with failure and disappointment (4)

Unsure how to evaluate myself as an evangelist (3)

Concerns About Pastoral Skills	*52*	*9.9*

How to be more effective as a caller (11)

How to persuade people to join the church (11)

How to lead training workshops (6)

Need for resource materials (4)

How to be a more effective worship leader (4)

How to make an authentic gospel appealing (4)

How to prepare people for church membership (3)

How to be a more effective preacher (2)

How to invite people to church (2)

How to evangelize without imposing (2)

How to use mass media in evangelism (1)

How to identify opportunities for evangelism (1)

How to identify people's needs (1)

Equipping and Motivating Church Members	*109*	*20.8*

How to equip church members for evangelism (27)

How to nurture their spiritual growth (14)

How to motivate church members re evangelism (14)

How to deal with people's fears about evangelism (12)

How to teach communication skills (10)

How to involve church officers in evangelism (9)

How to increase their sense of The Church (6)

How to involve the passive church-goer (5)

How to teach visitation skills to lay people (5)

How to increase their sense of mission (2)

How to avoid "overkill" (2)

How to help people discover their gifts (2)

How to do evangelism in the church school (1)

Evangelism Programs for the Local Church	*60*	*11.4*

How to reach and serve the community (23)

How to involve the congregation in the community (10)

Looking for new program ideas, techniques (7)

An evangelistic program for the small church (5)

An evangelistic program for the suburban church (5)

Category	Number	Percent
An evangelistic program for the urban church (4)		
An evangelistic program for the rural church (3)		
How to grow through visitation evangelism (3)		
Reaching the Unchurched	*30*	*5.7*
How to reach and minister to the unchurched (8)		
How to reach unchurched youth (6)		
How to tell if someone is receptive or resistant (5)		
How to approach various minority groups (4)		
Who and what is an "outsider"? (2)		
How to reach the unchruched poor (1)		
How to reach and minister to the aged (1)		
How to minister to those with special needs (1)		
How to reach middle-aged people (1)		
How to reach men (1)		
Ministering to Inactive Members	*27*	*5.1*
How to keep them from becoming inactive (12)		
How to reach those who are inactive (7)		
What is the church officers' role in the process (3)		
How to keep young people active in the church (2)		
How to revive the indifferent (2)		
Coping with the problems of growth (1)		
Totals	525	100.0

Appendix B
Word Associations

Evangelism	Evangelism and You	Evangelism and the Average Church Member
airports	* apprehensive	* afraid
altar call	* avoid	* anti-evangelism
ambassador	bearer of truth	* apathetic
Billy Graham	care, caring	* apprehensive
caring	change	* bigness
Christ	commission	Billy Graham
church	concern	calling
commitment	* doubts	* caricature
communication	enthusiasm	* cold
conversion	* failure	conversion
decision	* frustration	* don't know how
* emotionalism	* gimmicks	* doubt
evangel	guide	eating
faith	* guilt	* embarrassed
good news	help	* emotionalism
gospel	Holy Spirit	evangelism-church
growth	* inadequate	* exclusive
Holy Spirit	* inconvenient	* forget it!
hope	* ineffective	* get money
incarnation	integrity	* ignorant
invitation	model	* inadequate
love	necessary	interested, but
mission	opportunity	membership
mystery	preaching	neighbors
necessary	professional	* overpowering

*Words with negative overtones.

Evangelism	Evangelism and You	Evangelism and the Average Church Member
people	prospects	* pastor's job
personal	questions	* procrastinate
preaching	relationships	revival
presence	servant	somebody else's job
proclamation	service	* threatened
reaching out	* somebody else's job	* time-consuming
reconciliation	sowing seeds	* uncomfortable
risk	* time-consuming	* undesirable
serving	visiting	* unequipped
sharing		* uninformed
street corners		* unnecessary
teaching		* what is it?
telling		* who me?
testimony		
tracts		
trust		
TV evangelists		
witness		

---

*Words with negative overtones

Notes

1. John R. W. Stott, *Christian Mission in the Modern World* (Inter-Varsity Press, 1976), Chapter II.

2. In all these definitions I have taken the liberty of substituting inclusive language where appropriate, and for the sake of consistency I have tried to follow a uniform pattern of capitalization.

3. In his very useful book *Introduction to Evangelism* (Broadman Press, 1983), Delos Miles places Niles's pithy saying in its proper context and discusses it along with other selected definitions.

4. Urban T. Holmes, III, *Turning to Christ: A Theology of Renewal and Evangelization* (Seabury Press, 1981), pp. 126–127.

5. C. Peter Wagner, *Your Church Can Grow* (Regal Books, 1976), p. 12. Donald McGavran is the recognized founder of the Church Growth Movement.

6. Donald McGavran's rejoinder to his critics needs to be heard: "The basic positions of church growth are profoundly biblical and theological, but are not a complete theology. Complete *your* theology by building these basic growth concepts as to urgency and authority of evangelism into it. As you set forth church growth theory and theology for your congregations and your denomination, use your own creedal statements, your own system. *Your church growth theology is your patois.* Do not attack church growth as theologically inadequate. Make it adequate according to the doctrines emphasized by your branch of the Church" (*Understanding Church Growth,* rev. ed., p. 8; Wm. B. Eerdmans Publishing Co., 1980).

7. Wagner, *Your Church Can Grow,* Chapter 10.

8. Ibid., Chapter 4. The theme of this chapter has been explored much more thoroughly in Wagner's book *Leading Your Church to Growth* (Regal Books, 1984).

9. Articles by sixteen of the participants were published in an interesting volume edited by Dean R. Hoge and David A. Roozen, entitled

Understanding Church Growth and Decline, 1950–1978 (Pilgrim Press, 1979).

10. Ibid., p. 326.

11. Ibid., p. 324.

12. McGavran, *Understanding Church Growth,* p. 198.

13. Wagner, *Your Church Can Grow,* p. 110.

14. Ibid., p. 158.

15. Donald P. Smith, *Congregations Alive* (Westminster Press, 1981).

16. Wagner, *Leading Your Church to Growth,* p. 28.

17. Eddie Gibbs, *I Believe in Church Growth* (Wm. B. Eerdmans Publishing Co., 1982), p. 125.

18. Ibid., p. 70.

19. Ibid., p. 80.

20. For a more complete commentary on Gibbs's book, see my review in *The Princeton Seminary Bulletin,* Vol. IV, No. 3, New Series, 1983.

21. Peter Wagner, for instance, devoted a chapter to the kingdom of God in a later book, *Church Growth and the Whole Gospel* (Harper & Row, 1981).

22. Lesslie Newbigin has given a penetrating analysis of Church Growth theology in Chapter 9 of his book *The Open Secret* (Wm. B. Eerdmans Publishing Co., 1978).

23. John Calvin, *Institutes of the Christian Religion,* translated by Henry Beveridge (Wm. B. Eerdmans Publishing Co., 1953), iv. iii. 4, Vol. II, pp. 318f.

24. George Sweazey has defined the possibilities very well in his excellent book *The Church as Evangelist* (Harper & Row, 1978).

25. Newbigin, *The Open Secret,* p. 150.

26. Stott, *Christian Mission in the Modern World,* pp. 26ff.

27. For a fuller discussion of the relationship between social action and evangelism, see Stott, *Christian Mission in the Modern World,* Chapter I, and my book *Service Evangelism* (Westminster Press, 1983 updated edition), pp. 58–63.

28. *Service Evangelism,* pp. 26–29.

29. Ibid., p. 53. My original expression was "sharing one's faith with them," which suggests that it is the evangelist who does all the talking. For that reason I eliminated the word "one's," so that it now reads "sharing faith with them," to emphasize that the sharing is a two-way process. The effective witness is the one who encourages others to share

their faith. This point is made in Addendum 3 on p. 199 of the second printing.

30. NCC Governing Board, Atlanta, Georgia, spring, 1976.

31. WCC, "A Theological Reflection."

32. WCC, "Theological Reflections," Vol. VII, No. 2.

33. In his article "Good News to the Poor," which appeared as part of *Your Kingdom Come—Mission Perspectives,* the Report on the World Conference on Mission and Evangelism, Melbourne, Australia, May 12–25, 1980, Raymond Fung appeals for an evangelism that views the poor not just as sinners but as the "sinned against." See also Harvie M. Conn, *Evangelism: Doing Justice and Preaching Grace* (Zondervan, 1982); Orlando E. Costas, *The Integrity of Mission: The Inner Life and Outreach of the Church* (Harper & Row, 1979); Ronald J. Sider, *Rich Christians in an Age of Hunger* (Inter-Varsity Press, 1977); Alan Walker, *The New Evangelism* (Abingdon Press, 1975); Jim Wallis, *The Call to Conversion* (Harper & Row, 1983); and Waldron Scott, *Bring Forth Justice* (Wm. B. Eerdmans Publishing Co., 1980), and *Serving Our Generation* (World Evangelical Fellowship, 1980).

34. Dean M. Kelley, *Why Conservative Churches Are Growing* (Harper & Row, 1977 updated edition), p. 37.

35. Ibid., p. 45.

36. Stott, *Christian Mission in the Modern World,* pp. 42ff.

37. Ibid., p. 53.

38. Walter Rauschenbusch, *A Theology for the Social Gospel* (Macmillan, 1917; repr. Abingdon), p. 133.

39. Ibid., p. 140.

40. C. Peter Wagner has addressed the topic of the relationship of pastoral and lay leadership to church membership growth in his book *Leading Your Church to Growth* (see Note 8).

41. See Matt. 4:23–24, 8:5–7, 8:16, 9:35, 12:9–15, 12:22, 14:14, 15: 21–28, 15:30, 19:2, 21:14; Mark 1:32–34, 1:40–42, 2:3–12, 3:1–5; Luke 4:40, 5:15, 6:17–19, 7:2–10, 9:37–42, 13:10–17, 14:1–6; et al.

42. *The Book of Common Worship* (Board of Christian Education of the Presbyterian Church in the U.S.A., 1946), p. 249.

43. Ibid., p. 228. The italics are mine.

44. *The Book of Order* (Offices of the General Assembly, UPCUSA and PCUS, 1981), G-14.0510.

45. *The Book of Common Worship,* p. 227.

46. No religion is true in and of itself, as Karl Barth has shown in his famous attack on religion in *Church Dogmatics* (Allenson, 1936–69), Vol. I, pp. 280–361. For Barth, all religion is unbelief. Christianity

falls under the same judgment as other religions, because it too is guilty of idolatry and self-righteousness. Yet Barth can assert that Christianity is the true religion, because Jesus Christ is the truth. That assertion is a statement of faith, given only by revelation. Without Jesus Christ there would be no Christianity. It possesses no reality of its own. It is the true religion only because of divine election, justification, and sanctification.

47. This is an Anselmian understanding of knowledge, which for Anselm was always faith in search of understanding *(fides quarens intellectum)*.

48. Vincent M. Bilotta III, unpublished manuscript entitled "The Displacement of the Spiritual with the Domain of the Psychological," January 8, 1975.

49. C. Samuel Calian, *Today's Pastor in Tomorrow's World* (Hawthorn Books, 1977), Chapter 7.

50. See *Service Evangelism*, Chapter 6, for a fuller discussion of the importance of listening in interpersonal witnessing.

51. Wayne Rice, *Junior High Ministry* (Zondervan, 1978), p. 31.

52. For some helpful suggestions on the art of sharing personal stories and linking them with The Story, see Roy Fairchild's *Lifestory Conversations*, one of the Good News Evangelism Booklet series published by the Program Agency of The United Presbyterian Church U.S.A. See also *The Reluctant Witness* by Kenneth L. Chafin (Broadman Press, 1975), especially Chapter 3, for a Southern Baptist perspective on the same subject.

53. George G. Hunter III, ed., *Rethinking Evangelism* (Tidings, 1971), Chapter 5, "How to Speak in the Open Air."

54. These terms are explained and diagrammed in *Service Evangelism*, pp. 85–86.

55. In his book *The Contagious Congregation* (Abingdon Press, 1979), George G. Hunter III has devoted a chapter to the subject of communicating the gospel to "resistant secular people" and a chapter to a strategy for reaching receptive people. He defines resistant people as "folks who, at least for now, are not open to a life-change, do not 'have the ears' to really hear the gospel—the kind of people William Booth characterized as 'gospel proof' " (p. 80).

56. In his book *The Apathetic and Bored Church Member* (Pittsford, N.Y.: LEAD Consultants, 1976), John Savage offers a psychological analysis, based on 101 interviews, of the dynamics that occur in the life of once-active church members who become inactive.

57. See *Service Evangelism*, pp. 93–95.

58. Holmes, *Turning to Christ,* pp. 70–74 (see Note 4).

59. The quotation marks are in acknowledgment of John R. Hendrick's valuable little book *Opening the Door of Faith* (John Knox Press, 1977), which examines many aspects of the relationship between faith and evangelism.

60. For a more detailed discussion of interpersonal witnessing see *Service Evangelism,* Chapters 5 and 6. See also *Effective Evangelism* by George E. Sweazey (Harper & Row, 1976 revised edition); *Out of the Salt Shaker: Evangelism as a Way of Life* by Rebecca Manley Pippert (Inter-Varsity Press, 1979); *One-on-One Evangelism* by James H. Jauncey (Moody Press, 1978).

61. George Sweazey has presented a thorough description of what it means for the church to be the evangelist in his book *The Church as Evangelist* (see Note 24).

Index